MEMORIES OF BUCKINGHAMSHIRE

by Martin Tapsell

Published by

Mercia Cinema Society,
(Publications Group),
64 Somerton Drive,
Erdington,
Birmingham,
West Midlands,
B23 5ST.

ISBN 0 946406 03 0

Designed by Chris Clegg

Typeset by Chris Wigg and printed by Galataprint,
Wolverhampton.

THE CREDITS

No book such as this could have been written without the help of people whose memory or expertise transcends my own. Some information received unfortunately fell outside the scope of the text as defined elsewhere. I am nevertheless grateful to those people who wrote to me about such early precursors of the cinema proper as the hut on an Aylesbury fairground with the grass floor. Those who contributed to the final text in various ways, are, in alphabetical order :—

R. Betteridge, Gerald Bignell, Sydney Brooks, Mrs. M.F. Brum, George Butler, Cecil Checkley, Steve Child, D.G. Cole of Rank Theatres, G.A. Coombes of Thorn EMI, Terry Deane, Wally Dent, Miss Derry French (who loaned a typewriter), Les Goldman, Granada Theatres, Leon Higgs, Wing Cdr. Charles Kimber, Jim Lambert, E. Legg, Roy Legg, Brian Leslie, Derek Lovell, Joe Marsh, Tony Mills, Jack Parkes, Mrs. Nora Podbury, S.V. Rixon, Keith Skone, Mrs. P. Spater, Mrs. Phyllis Spuffard, Mrs. Daisy Stringer, Roger Tear, G.F. Warner, A.H. Wigley, Alec Williams, Frank Wilson, Len Wright and not forgetting Anita, who showed me round Zetters' Club in Wolverton.

In addition, many private individuals and the cinema circuits kindly provided photographs, which are acknowledged individually. I can hardly omit either the contribution of colleagues on the staff of Bucks County Library, too numerous to name, who have assisted greatly by sending me press cuttings on local cinemas, or suggested persons I might contact in their local areas. They have maintained their interest in the progress of the book, as have several county newspapers, who have given space to reporting the project, or given permission for me to consult files of their newspapers. Hopefully, you will all find this little history interesting, and readers, please do not hesitate to send me any further information you may have, as the time to document cinema history is NOW — before it is too late!

Martin Tapsell

INTRODUCTION

Most people will have memories, however distant, of seeing a film on the big screen of their local cinema. But what about the building? Was it a sumptuous masterpiece of thirties design, visited in its heyday, or a tatty disgrace of a picture house with peeling stucco, whose manager anxiously scanned the ice cream returns? Either extreme, from luxurious dream palace to bug hut, could attract loyal patronage week after week, many escaping from a world harsher than we know today. By 1939, 5,500 such darkened places were showing films, the art form of the twentieth century, in buildings that brought a new form of architecture to the planet.

At one time, the films exhibited were normally escapist, revealing to mainly working class audiences a world of undreamt wealth and opulence, to which, by implication, they should aspire. The emphasis in the fifties and sixties gradually shifted to more social realism, bringing a trend to more "adult" themes, rating an 'X' certificate. This drove away some of the public, who were simultaneously being wooed by fireside television and later, bingo. A long haemorrhage in the cinema industry began, which has not yet ceased, although the tourniquets of part-time bingo and subdivided auditoria have been applied where practicable. The latter expedient is not entirely satisfactory, even for those apparently quite immune from the typically British nostalgia for the old days. There is a sense of diminished occasion, viewing (I use that word advisedly) a big screen film in a hundred seat studio.

Nationally, we have lost a great deal of fine architecture, together with many palm festooned foyers, the ubiquitous uniformed commissionaires, the newsreel, the cafe, the organ and sometimes even the screen curtains. On the plus side, seating is more comfortable and better spaced, ventilation, sound and projection is vastly improved, and cinemagoers can encounter new facilities, such as licensed bars or space invaders! When the right film reaches the right audience and the presentation is good, that old magic that is cinema can still enchant loyal cinemagoers.

Thirty-one years ago, when 1,270,000,000 admissions were being recorded nationally, the county's largest town had four cinemas, seating between them 4,300, into which 24,000 people filed each week. They paid between 1/3d (6p) and 3/6d (17½p) for the privilege. 800 children alone could be expected at the Odeon each Saturday morning. I am referring to High Wycombe, where less than two decades later, the Palace became a solo situation, and, today even this survivor is likely to close soon according to press reports. In terms of film entertainment, as in public transport, we seem to have gone into reverse! The county has had a varied heritage in cinema architecture and even today one can witness the great variety of styles that evolved within a space of only 25 years, between say, the Electra, Newport Pagnell and the Odeon, Aylesbury. Before any more of the remaining eight go dark, it is time to tell their story, with the help of those who were entertained in them or who actually worked in this endangered species.

The main part of this booklet consists of an alphabetical gazetteer of Buckinghamshire towns and villages having a purpose-built cinema at any time, or any other public hall used for cinematographic entertainment over several years, thus meriting a listing in the cinema buffs' bible, the Kinematograph Yearbook. Films were of course shown in innumerable other halls, the Woburn Sands Social Club and Lane End Village Hall (where Ministry of Information films were screened in World War II) being two typical examples. However, the bona fide cinemas are interesting and diverse enough in themselves, and it should be possible to run the gamut from the "super show" to that equally rare (nowadays) phenomenon, the draughty flea pit.

THE CINEMA IN BUCKINGHAMSHIRE -- SOME MAIN EVENTS

1909   First Palace Cinema opens in High Wycombe.

1911   Purpose-built cinemas open in Aylesbury (Market Theatre), Fenny Stratford (Palace) and Wolverton (Palace).

1912   More cinemas open at Chesham (Empire), High Wycombe (Electroscope) and Newport Pagnell (Electric), but a fire destroys Palace, High Wycombe.

1913   Grand, High Wycombe opened.

1914   Three more Palaces open at Gold Hill, Chesham and Marlow, plus Farnham Common Cinema.

1915   Burnham Electric opens.

1917   Town Hall, Aylesbury begins to show films.

1918   Scala, Stony Stratford opened.

1919   Electric, Olney opens in New Hall.

1921   First films shown in Oddfellows' Hall, Winslow.

1922   Pavilion, Amersham and Second Palace at High Wycombe opened.

1924   Fire guts Aylesbury Market Theatre but it is re-built.

1925   New cinemas at Aylesbury (Grand Pavilion), Gerrards Cross (Playhouse - now Classic) and at Halton Camp.

1926   The Empire, Wolverton becomes a cinema and is used as a strikers HQ.

1927   Picture House, now Chiltern, Beaconsfield opened.

1928   Regent, Amersham opened, replacing Pavilion as cinema, also Plaza, Iver.

1930   Broadway, Chalfont St. Peter supersedes Gold Hill cinema. Majestic, later Odeon, High Wycombe opened.

1934   Last town to get a cinema (Bourne End) welcomes the Royalty, and Buckingham sees films in a purpose-built new cinema called the Chandos.

1936   Pavilion, Aylesbury enlarged and modernised. Studio, Bletchley opened. Former Pavilion, Amersham becomes Playhouse Theatre.

4

1937	Three towns get new cinemas — Aylesbury (Odeon), High Wycombe (Rex) and Chesham (Embassy).
1938	A new County Cinema at Marlow replaces the old Palace/County.
1940	An early closure — the Plaza, Iver becomes a furniture store.
1941	Al Bowlly plays the Rex, High Wycombe. County, Marlow renamed Odeon.
1944	Majestic, High Wycombe also renamed Odeon.
1947	It's no harder to say Granada — the new name of the Pavilion, Aylesbury.
1952	A small town cinema closed — the Electric, Olney.
1954	Last play at the County, Aylesbury, formerly the Market Theatre/Cinema.
1956	Winslow sees its last film, and Amersham its last play at the Playhouse.
1957	Rank closes its elderly property at Fenny Stratford — the County.
1959	Shipman & King close their Astoria (ex Palace), Chesham, Rank dispose of Odeon, Marlow which is renamed Regal and Royalty, Bourne End closed.
1960	Beaconsfield U.D.C. take bold step of buying their cinema.
1961	Scala, Stony Stratford and Palace, Wolverton close on the same day.
1962	More closures at Regent, Amersham and Grand, High Wycombe.
1963	Picture House, Beaconsfield renamed Chiltern.
1965	High Wycombe's newest cinema, the Rex closes down.
1968	Chandos, Buckingham introduces part-time bingo.
1969	High Wycombe loses its atmospheric Odeon and Wolverton's last cinema, the Empire becomes a Post Office sorting office.
1972	Granada, Aylesbury closes in favour of full-time bingo. County, Fenny Stratford finally demolished.
1973	First multiple in Bucks opens — the Odeon, tripled in Aylesbury.
1979	A ghost starts to haunt the Chiltern, Beaconsfield. The Classic, Gerrards Cross becomes a twin.
1982	Embassy, Chesham closes but the Electra, Newport Pagnell celebrates its 70th anniversary. High Wycombe's cinema due to close within months.

SOME WARTIME MEMORIES IN SOUTH BUCKS

The Second World War had a number of effects on cinemas. There was a sudden halt to the building boom, neon and other external lighting had to be extinguished, and many of the male staff were called up. However, the escapist value of the cinema was soon recognised as an invaluable aid to morale during those six years of continual stress. Audiences swelled despite the hazards of negotiating darkened, rubble-strewn streets. The county escaped the worst of the blitz, but the southern half in particular was not immune from danger. A projectionist at the now permanently darkened Palace, High Wycombe, remembers the usherettes proceeding quietly to the exits when the alarm went, a special record being played, and the invitation to any member of the audience who wished to leave. The programme then resumed, many preferring to remain in the comforting darkness, rather than face the journey to their homes or the nearest shelter. Things were worst for the projectionist high up in the building (no ground floor minis in those days). He or she would hear bombs crumping all around, but far from street level, the roof would need special attention in case incendiaries needed to be thrown off.

A few cinemas closed to meet the lucrative demand for storage space for furniture during the time road freight was severely restricted. The short lived Plaza, Iver, was a local example of a cinema to take on this new role. The remainder often never had it so good, audiences being swollen by wartime evacuees, as at Amersham, or by nearby army camps like the one close to Bourne End. The blitz also meant that entertainers were willing to escape from London to perform for quite modest fees. We have already referred to Al Bowlly at the Rex, High Wycombe, but John Watsham, who acquired this cinema in August, 1938, booked many other acts, including Turner Layton, Monte Crick and the Western Brothers (who were actually cousins). The top fee he paid (to Hutch) was £125. When Chaplin's film, *The Great Dictator*, came out Charlie stipulated that the film must be shown open market, but with no other film other than newsreels and adverts in tandem. United Artists were surprised when Mr. Watsham asked to take the film concurrently with the Odeon under these conditions. However, the Rex offered live acts as the supporting feature, including the Eileen Winterton trio. However these ladies were shocked to be billed as the "Knickerbocker Glories" -- boy can they can-can! However, by the end of a great week they were coming round to the idea of using the name. The Odeon did well with the overflow, although Chaplin thought he had literally been upstaged, and scrutinised the contracts more closely after that.

1939-45 was therefore not a time of expansion or innovation for the cinema, but the forties were the last decade of mass popularity for the cinema, the like of which was never seen again. Nowadays the cinema seems to be becoming as scarce as repertory theatres! Anyone who wishes to read a good account of cinemas under fire should refer to Edward Guy Trice Morgan's book 'Red roses every night' which was published by Quality Press in 1948. What happened to just one circuit, (Granada), in the metropolis makes fascinating reading.

AMERSHAM

Amersham-on-the-Hill is the young offshoot of the old town in the valley below. The modern town is centred around and above the Metropolitan line terminus.

From the extremity of the down platform at the west end of the tube station, one can look down on the roof of a modestly proportioned building which now serves as Auction rooms for Pretty & Ellis. However, the building has a long pedigree, which is belied by the recent brick alterations to the frontage. This was once the Bijou Hall, which existed from at least 1907 onwards. Equipped with a stage, it was used for various purposes including dancing. The first date when we know films began to be shown on a regular basis was 1922, when the hall was re-christened the Pavilion and run as a cinema and theatre by Walter Collins. The Pavilion opened on 18th November, 1922 with a concert party and play, and the first film followed 5 days later on the 23rd (Thursday). This, incidentally, was called *Forbidden Fruit* — billed as a gorgeous romance of married life.

Mr. Collins had started life as a pianist and composer, which must have enhanced the quality of the musical entertainment on offer. The silent films were accompanied by a piano, with the addition of drums for the real blockbusters! The Pavilion only seated 150 on one floor, but had all the trappings of larger halls. There was a commissionaire in navy blue uniform to welcome the patrons, and downstairs, Mrs. Collins ran an attractively furnished cafe. Among the cafe's wares was a large selection of chocolates at prices which would seem incredible today. The cafe's dishes, commonplace enough then, are antique collectors' items today. Confectionery known as candy kisses were sold during the intervals, which were no doubt much sought after by the children attending matinees of *Rin Tin Tin* and the original version of *Felix the Cat*. Children of the less well off were treated to an annual Christmas party in the cafe — one hopes they could afford the few pence required to gain admission throughout the rest of the year.

After the Regent opened in 1928, the Pavilion dropped films entirely, but remained open for theatrical productions. The last film shown here was on 1st December, 1928. To confuse the historian, the theatre re-opened after a period of closure, as the Playhouse, on Boxing Day, 1936. Sally Latimer, the new proprietor, extended the hall backwards, increasing the capacity to 240, and particularly in the war years (when Amersham's population was swollen by evacuees) business boomed. The Playhouse was for a time the only live theatre in the whole county, until Aylesbury's re-opened in 1948. Attendances fell away after television caught hold, and the proximity of the West End did not help the box office. The last proprietors — John Ferris and his wife, Rosa De Leon, were, despite their dedication, unable to make the theatre pay. After the 1955/56 pantomime season, the Playhouse closed and its contents were sold off in an act of finality. There seems to have been a planning application for use as a plastics factory, but in the event, the local auctioneers, Pretty & Ellis took over the venerable property. The public are still admitted on sale days.

Mr. Collins teamed up with a local builder, Alfred Woodley of Lexham

Gardens to form a new company, Colwood Pictures and Theatres Ltd. Their combined expertise resulted in the construction of a new cinema in Sycamore Road. Apart from the Regent, Amersham, it is not without interest that Woodley's also built the Rivoli at Ruislip, which was also to pass to the Shipman & King circuit and suffer the same fate, albeit four years later. In 1928, the Regent cinema must have been particularly imposing, being the largest building in a semi built-up road. The stability of two elm trees growing on waste land opposite gave rise to some concern during the erection of the cinema. The Regent was faced mainly in stone, with seven short pillars flanking the first floor windows. The entrance, which had no canopy, was approached by a short flight of steps leading to four pairs of double doors. External publicity and lighting was restrained. The former was limited to poster panels integral to the frontage design and the name Regent above the pillars. Apart from spotlights over the poster panels, two lanterns flanked the entrance and a third one, perched, beacon-like on the roof. Until the Second World War, a row of shaded bulbs illuminated the main entrance. The overall design of this cinema was carried out by F.C. Mitchell. The interior of the Regent was nothing if not opulent, with richly ornamented gilt and cream plaster work and thick pile carpets over which walked an immaculately dressed commissionaire in red and gold braid. Star portraits in black frames adorned the walls of the foyer and staircases.

AMERSHAM REGENT Messrs Podbury (projectionist) and Oakley (doorman) stand outside about 1930
Photo: Mrs Norah Podbury

On 3rd December, 1928, the Regent opened its doors to the first patrons who, 658 at a time, could see Sir Harry Lauder in *The Hunting Tower*. Perhaps the slogan 'you can't go wrong if you follow the throng' worked for a time, but the plush red seats did not draw enough patrons to prevent Colwood Pictures selling out quite soon to Shipman & King. Mr. Collins subsequently became musical director of the De La Warr Pavilion, Bexhill, which boasted a 32 piece orchestra. The 'finest cinema in Bucks' as the *Bucks Examiner* termed it, was converted to sound without difficulty. About the same time, the 30-feet deep stage facilities came into their own during a period of closure at the Pavilion. In November, 1930, the Cestreham players presented *Iolanthe* at the Regent. There were live performances about once a month, with well known stars like Jack Warner and sisters Gert and Daisy appearing. Attendances grew during the War, as at the Playhouse, and some years later, in 1955, a wide screen was installed. However, the writing was on the wall four years later when Shipman & King closed the nearby Astoria, Chesham. In the few months preceding the same closure decision in Amersham, attendances slumped at times to a mere 3 or 4 per performance. Closure was not unopposed however — the town had lost its theatre 6 years earlier, remember? A petition supported by such south Bucks notables as Dirk Bogarde (who once lived in Beel House) and Margaret Rutherford, was circulated. Dirk Bogarde favoured a mixed policy of repertory plus quality films like *A Taste of Honey*. Backers of the "save the Regent" plan met at the *Bucks Examiner's* office, those present including Pat Moss, the rally driver. After the cinema closed on 10th March, 1962, the campaign was taken to a Ministry enquiry, which however, sanctioned a change of designated use for the site. The Regent was quickly demolished and a supermarket built on the site. As the local press wryly remarked, *Breakfast at Tiffany's* (the last picture show) was now giving way to breakfast cereals. The last manager, 25 year-old Alex Budden, returned to the Regent, Waltham Cross whence he came, after playing a prominent part in the cinema-theatre campaign.

AYLESBURY

The County town, 40 miles from London, much altered and expanded in the last 20 years.

As would be expected, Aylesbury was one of the first towns to get a purpose-built cinema. In the case of the Market Theatre, off Market Square, it had a theatre as well. The first building on the site opened on 21st January, 1911, showing animated pictures of short duration supported by variety artistes, the first of whom was Kathleen Basley, the contralto. Advertised as "the family house where everyone visits", the original proprietors were Messrs. Freeman and Whitcher, who formed the Aylesbury Electric Company. Films were then billed according to length, the Bucks Herald showing films of 3,000 feet or more, like *His Little Lordship* in heavy type, and shorts like *Captain Jinks' Getaway* in ordinary type. For the first 13 years the hall seated 650 including the balcony, in an auditorium measuring 61 x 38½ feet wide.

AYLESBURY MARKET The narrow entrance seen in its last year, September 1980.
Photo: Martin Tapsell

A fire on Easter Saturday, 19th April, 1924, gutted all but the foyer and the manager's office, but re-building was quickly undertaken, the new building seating 725 despite the omission of a balcony. The theatre re-opened on 22nd December, 1924 with *The Telephone Girl*. Stage facilities were improved with a 34½ x 25 feet deep stage and better dressing rooms. The auditorium had a barrel vaulted ceiling with ornamental ribs designed by architects Taylor and White of Bourbon Street and executed by local builders Webster and Cannon of Cambridge Street. Films continued to be shown until at least the end of 1937, by which time sound had been installed, the first talkie, *The Jazz Singer*, being shown in April, 1929. The Market Theatre changed hands becoming part of the Wainwright circuit and subsequently London & District Cinemas in 1937.

In the Second World War, the theatre was closed by 1940 and used for storage, not re-opening until 19th September, 1947, but this time with repertory only. From May, 1948 until 13th March, 1954 it was known as the County Theatre, the last play of all being *The Blue Goose* — the nearest title to The White Duck perhaps? On 18th May, 1954, a Hammond Organ was heard accompanying skaters and dancers in the "Grosvenor", but bingo was also on offer. The fire which wrecked the town hall resulted in a final name change and even greater variety when the Borough Assembly Halls started life in October, 1963. Superseded in 1975 by the new Civic Centre, the old theatre ended its life as a social club for CBS, a large Aylesbury-based firm. As such it survived until October, 1980, when demolition men working on the big Hale Leys shopping centre got to grips with the Market Theatre. My last memory of it is seeing bulldozers crashing around the roofless auditorium, balloons from the last CBS party still semi-inflated on the walls.

The second place of screen entertainment was the Town Hall, which was originally built off Market Square as the Corn Exchange in 1864-65. Built in late Elizabethan style in red brick with stone facings, the main hall was 90 feet long and 45 feet wide. Thirty-eight feet above the floor, a roof supported by semicircular iron ribs and spandrils filled with tracery, provided daylight through a 70 feet skylight. Offices were sandwiched between the supporting buttresses. Unlike a proper cinema, there was a gallery at each end.

Mrs. Charles Senior presented films there from 25th May, 1917, the first one for the record being *His Last Dollar*. The Seniors were well disposed towards ex-servicemen, reserving part of their press space for appeals for work on behalf of old soldiers returning from the Great War. Old age pensioners too benefited from free admission on Friday nights. Films continued from Thursdays to Saturdays shown on a screen measuring 17 x 12½ feet, interrupted occasionally by the need to use the Town Hall for other functions including counting votes. The General Purposes Committee became increasingly disturbed about the single exit from the gallery, wanting this closed to film audiences. However the Seniors opened their Grand Pavilion (see page 12) in March, 1925, so that the fire regulations hardly had time to affect business before films ceased that June. From then on, the Town Hall continued in use for a variety of civic entertainment until it was irreparably damaged by fire in 1962.

The Seniors, who had already been exhibiting films in the Town Hall for 8 years, brought the purpose-built cinema to Aylesbury when their Grand Pavilion opened in the High Street on 2nd March, 1925. Here, 1,000 patrons could be seated in an auditorium designed in the neo-Grecian style by Aylesbury architect C.H. Wright. The decor was muted buff and white, with colour contributed by the pink pedestals with their purple dados. Outside, the entrance was classical in appearance with a stepped gable and single suspended globe. A long foyer led in from the main street, but such comforts as a drying room for wet overcoats and even a reading and writing room were provided before the patrons reached the auditorium. A wireless set and transport timetables were also provided for their diversion. Films were shown nightly with matinees on Wednesdays and Saturdays, starting with *A Boy of Flanders*. Apart from the 20 x 15 feet screen, there was a large stage and even a musicians' balcony half-way down the auditorium.

AYLESBURY PAVILION Exterior with a mammoth cut-out display, 1929
Interior view of the Pavilion taken in 1936
Photo: Premier Bioscope, Sutton

Abbreviated to the Pavilion, the cinema passed into the same hands as the Market Theatre (see page 9). In October, 1936 it closed when the auditorium was extended to the plans of Robert Cromie, on behalf of the directors J.G., G.M. and R.B. Wainwright. The extension at the screen end brought seating capacity up to 1,234, whilst the stage itself measured 51 x 23 feet deep, with dressing rooms provided. As described in the January, 1937 issue of *Cinema & Theatre Construction*, the Pavilion was transformed internally. Among the many new features included was a new staircase to the balcony to the right of the stalls doors and a proscenium arch enriched by a coved surround decorated by Lois Ososki's sprayed on drawings. The seating was upholstered in a rubberised moquette of old rose colour with mahogany frames. New air conditioning equipment capable of dealing with 200,000 cubic feet of air every 15 minutes was installed, also a much more powerful boiler plant. The old

projection room was retained, but with the addition of an exterior staircase. The Grecian style frontage was replaced by a tall brick elevation faced in cream terrazzo with a central rectangular window illuminated from behind and surrounded by green tiles. This window was purely decorative, being above the level of the foyer.

The rebuilt cinema was opened again on 4th January, 1937. Just over ten years later, in June, 1947, the Pavilion changed its name to Granada after passing to the circuit of that name. The slogan was, "It's no harder to say Granada!" Granada then had some 45 cinemas compared with a handful showing films today. Both before and after the change of ownership, live shows were periodically held, two examples being Aylesbury Operatic Society's production of *Rose Marie* in March, 1937, or the appearance of likeable twerp Bernard ("I only arsked") Bresslaw on stage in the fifties. As late as April, 1971, Sid Lawrence and his orchestra were evoking the big band sound. However, by then Granada were turning increasingly towards bingo, and submitted plans for part-time bingo in this theatre in March, 1971. However, as the Granada was by then only breaking even financially, it was decided to drop films entirely. Thus it was that Clint Eastwood was the last star to visit the screen as *Joe Kidd* on 7th October, 1972.

Early next year, Liberal gourmet, Clement Freud was invited to open Granada's 20th bingo club, over which the last cinema manager, Steve Waddingham remained as administrations manager. Today, the stalls seating has been replaced by cafeteria-style tables, the box is an equipment store, and the 200 retained cinema seats in the balcony are used mainly on "snowball" or other special nights. The stage has gone, but cabaret acts are still engaged at the close of the sessions. The old cinema is well cared for and clean, and currently decorated in chocolate with beige cream wallpapered panels. There are about 60 employees, whose staff accommodation is on the right of the auditorium, plus the plenum and boiler plant. On the High Street side, an extension for 100 prize bingo players was built in 1979. Having rather a shallow balcony, the Granada had less potential for sub-division than the Odeon (see page 15) and by one account its acoustics for films were not ideal in some parts of the hall. However, the Granada Club is arguably the best appointed club of its kind in the county and receives good support from players of both sexes.

AYLESBURY GRANADA In March 1966 advertising the Royal Ballet film. Opposite, the auditorium in March 1966.
Photos: Photo Coverage Ltd., Copyright: Granada Theatres

On 15th July, 1937, *Ideal Kinema* reported the arrival of Aylesbury's latest, and final cinema. The heading 'Glass Fronted Odeon at Aylesbury' referred to the new polished substance containing a glass aggregate used for the fins and base of the frontage, whilst the main frontage was faced with cream glass faced with jade green trimmings. Sited on high land in Cambridge Street, the cinema is most prominent from Station Street or the approaches from Bierton. Designed for Oscar Deutsch by Andrew Mather, who, unlike the circuit chief, was able to be present at the opening ceremony on 21st June, 1937. This was performed by the Earl of Courtdown with the band of the Second battalion, the Cameronians in support, the opening film being *Dimples*, starring child star Shirley Temple. The seating capacity was originally 1,451, with 954 in the stalls plus 497 in the circle.

The Odeon has a lofty entrance hall, originally painted green finished with gold, and lit by a large day light in the ceiling which is now painted over. The *Bucks Herald* found the auditorium to be staid, almost severe, but it has escaped the modernisation which befalls many earlier and more decorative interiors. Then, as now, the sloping, cream coloured ceiling was broken up at intervals by cross-over troughs, ornamented by ribbed plastic treatment, behind which are housed concealed lighting. A continuous decorative grille extending from the side walls and over the ceiling focuses attention on the proscenium and serves as the extract mechanism for the ventilation plant. The original colour scheme

AYLESBURY ODEON
Photos: John Maltby

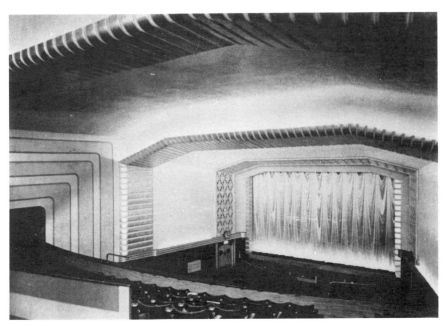

must have been pleasing — the green crushed velvet seating blending admirably with the autumn tints of the carpet design according to *Ideal Kinema*. The Holophane stage lighting still gives pleasing colour changes on the curtains before Screen 1 performances today.

In 1937, the Odeon charged 9d, 1/- or 1/3d for stalls seats or 1/6d and 2/- in the balcony, compared with a top price of £2.20 today. From New Year's day, 1938, children had their own Saturday Mickey Mouse Club, which was given a send off with a congratulatory telegram from Oscar Deutsch before the audience settled down to a coronation film and a Ken Maynard Western. Over 35 years later children were again involved in a first day ceremony when the Odeon became a triple. Triplets were present on Sunday, 26th August, 1973 when the old circle became Screen 1 and a wall dropped down from the balcony rails provided two mini cinemas in the rear stalls. The conversion, which was achieved without closure to the public, cost £40,000, just £10,000 less than the whole building had cost in 1937! Seating capacity was reduced to 491 in Screen 1, which remains much as it was originally, whilst Screens 2 and 3 seat 108 and 99 respectively. The minis are rather small, which means that spacing out the rows cannot be done without cutting capacity drastically. For evening performances, all seats in the minis are bookable, and it has been known for successful films to be sold out. At the time of the tripling, the projection suite was resited between the minis, whose screens are reached by mirror projection.

Further changes have occurred since 1973. In 1974 a trolley bar service started in the minis, and upstairs in the Screen 1 foyer, a new bar counter and seating was installed in 1981. On the debit side, a large tubular chandelier in the foyer went at the time the sales kiosk was replaced. Discerning patrons can still

17

see other features of interest including some original light fittings in Screen 1, the twin curved staircases with their multi-coloured rubber treads, a couple of art deco sofas, and at night the large red neon Odeon sign outside which is echoed in octagonal style lettering on the foyer tiles. The last cinema to open in Bucks, and the only one in the Rank circuit left in the county, business can range from poor to excellent, longish queues materialising in the school holidays and for certain films like *Arthur* which enjoyed a three month run during 1981.

BEACONSFIELD

A town whose Georgian crossroads contrasts with the more modern extension towards the railway station. It was made prosperous, first by stage coaches, and now by well-heeled commuters.

Beaconsfield's first cinema opened in Burkes Hall, which stood at the corner of Burkes and Gregories Roads. It is not certain just how soon films were shown in this public hall, which dated from 1911 and originally held dances, plays and other functions. There were certainly films in 1921, in which year the cinema closed for two months during which new lighting, a new dynamo and motor generator and a second projector were installed. The re-opening took place on 16th February, 1922.

BEACONSFIELD CHILTERN Taken in 1927
Photos: Kevin Wheelan

The proprietor of the first Picture House, as it was called, was Charles Cheshir, whose name will arise again in this survey. Owing to the popularity of Charlie Chaplin, the cinema was even called the Chaplin in press advertising for a time. It remained on films until the new Picture House, just a few yards down the road, was opened in 1927. Immediately thereafter, the Old Picture House advertised itself as the 'dance hall with the perfectly sprung floor'. Today the building no longer exists, but is commemorated on a plaque outside Cardain House. This block of shops and offices was built on the site in 1965.

The Picture House, 14 Station Road, took only six months to build at a cost of £14,000. The architects, J.R. Leathart and W.F. Grainger, designed the building in a Georgian style to blend with the then semi-rural character of the area. The frontage was faced with multi-coloured bricks and stone dressings with a steep pitched green slate roof. Its domestic character is emphasised by the restrained windows and the chimney stack, but the large arched stone entrance is reminiscent of public libraries of the period. Apparently there was some last minute alterations to the layout of the projection room and manager's accommodation, resulting in the General Purposes Committee approving a variation in the width of the pavement outside from 7 feet to 11 feet. Inside the style avoided unnecessary decorative treatment, leaning gently towards the Egyptian in the pilasters of the small foyer and the proscenium surround. The 500 seat, one floor auditorium, had a slightly curved ceiling relieved by two ventillating apertures. The builders of the Picture House were Wright's of Great Missenden.

The film shown on the opening night, 15th September, 1927, was *Mare Nostrum* to which admission was gained by a ticket ballot. The cinema had a succession of proprietors — W.J. Smith, H.S. Morgan and Weller and Stevenson, who also operated the Carlton, Princes Risborough and Broadway, Chalfont St. Peter (see page 64). In 1960, Beaconsfield U.D.C. made a bold decision, for a town of only 10,000 people, of buying the cinema for £25,000. The motive was to acquire a venue for stage plays, which were to be held four weeks a year on the newly constructed stage. The present name, Chiltern Cinema, was used on 8th November, 1963, when the cinema re-opened after two weeks of redecoration by Modernisation Ltd. The council-run cinema did not become profitable for several years, 1968 being the first year in which an overall profit (£1.330) was made, including a healthy rise of £356 over the previous year in the sale of ices and confectionery.

The Chiltern's manager at this time was Walter Gay, who by astute programming, enticed children from as far as Slough and Uxbridge to see films like *Snow White*. Some readers may remember those plaintive faces outside cinemas showing an A certificate who pleaded: "Take us in Mister? You don't have to sit with us!" In the days before AA certificates, many 'A's' were innocuous enough compared with the danger of children meeting dubious adult company outside. Realising this, Mr. Gay tried to get the General Purposes Committee to relax admission restrictions. Failing to get a local dispensation, Mr. Gay made the gesture of taking in whole droves of children into a reserved area and sitting with them — there was no stipulation in the regulations as to how many children could accompany the adult, or what relationship the adult must have to the child. Thus local children saw *Battle of Anzio* with Mr. Gay to the accompaniment of much press interest. Present certificates have made this stratagem redundant.

The Chiltern reached a low ebb in 1974, patrons deserting to the greater comfort of the Classic, Gerrards Cross. Demolition was even mooted, with possible inclusion of a new mini cinema in the proposed civic centre. However, the crisis passed in 1978 when the Council decided to lease the Chiltern to the Plaza (Margate) Ltd., initially for two years. John Scotchmer, who had recently left as manager, came back to Beaconsfield. Today, the re-seated and redecorated Chiltern with 277 seats, is one of the county's more successful cinemas, which includes late night shows on Saturday in its programming. An unusual venture of quite recent origin was when a local home movie retailer hired the cinema for free previews of Super 8 film, setting up their own projector at the back of the auditorium. Admission prices (in October, 1982) were £1.80 for adults for all seats. The manager's flat adjacent to the projection room with separate street access, is still occupied, currently by a young lady manageress, Clair Matthews. Clair (21) who was formerly at the Plaza, Margate, was faced with an unusual problem. A former manager, thought to be Walter Gay, still takes a posthumous interest in the cinema. Objects move around in the flat, doors slam, and in the cinema, the doors have been found wide open in the morning, although still chained. Worse still perhaps, the curtains mysteriously closed during the screening of the *Exorcist*. Perhaps the ghost thought it would give the manageress ideas! The chief result of this supernatural activity is that there are plenty of openings for usherettes, who tend to leave after seeing the ghost alone in the cinema at night.

BLETCHLEY AND FENNY STRATFORD

Bletchley was formerly a small village much expanded into a 'town of trains' by the coming of the railway. Fenny Stratford is a more historic town on Watling Street.

The County Cinema, which stood on Fenny High Street, had the distinction of being one of the first 50 provincial cinemas in the country, dated back as it did to 1911. The building was originally a Methodist chapel and Sunday school with adjacent burial ground. The Methodists moved to new quarters in Bletchley Road, selling the old chapel to Barber's Picture Palace Company. The Congleton born Alderman had the chapel and Sunday school knocked into one, retaining the gallery. Even some of the old pews stayed on — cinema goers did not expect plush seating in 1911! The actual first night was Monday, 16th October, 1911, making the Palace, as it was first known, the first cinema in north Bucks by a short head over the Palace, Wolverton (see page 70). The opening was arranged at such short notice that the decoration was incomplete, but the film *The Leading Lady* was shown without a breakdown. In support there was a 'beautifully coloured film' about the Keeki Falls. This was shown in hues ranging from pea-green to Sandhouse soup according to advertising. The audience at the change of programme on Thursday were not so lucky as their film was lost on the railway, and they had to be given refunds. From then on performances were held twice nightly at 7 and 9 p.m. excepting of course, Sundays.

A description of what is was like to see a film in the Palace in the early days could be equally applied, with minor variations, to the other pioneer picture palaces in Bucks. Patrons queued outside to pay their tuppences at a little pay box, then sat on hard forms until the lights suddenly went out — no dimmers in those days. The flickering film began in total silence except for the whirr of the hand cranked projector. Soon the footsteps of the lady pianist would be heard walking down to the front, passing behind her curtain in the manner of a church organist. The piano light would be switched on, the music sorted and the accompaniment improvised according to the nature of the film. There was a gas engine in the basement which worked the electric projector installed during the Great War.

The Palace seated 514 and it knew several proprietors before passing to County cinemas in 1927. These included Mr. Amos Stevenson of the Fenny Stratford Gas Company, and Mr. Alfred Jacob, a garage owner. The latter, who took over in 1920, bought up the remains of the Imperial Toilet Roll Co. next door, which had burned down in March, 1912, and erected a garage on the site. Under County Cinemas, the name changed first to Majestic, then by March, 1929 to King George's. At this period, the auditorium was enlarged, the staircases reconstructed and a new pay box installed. The cinema benefited from the arrival of a promotion-minded manager, Leslie Parsons, who brought in an effects man to supplement the pianist, and not content with that, added an orchestra.

In June, 1929, the long reign of his successor, J.J. Betteridge, M.I. Mech. E., began. Mr. Betteridge had been at the Lyric, Birmingham, and as an accomplished violinist, had played in many theatre and cinema orchestras. He was also a skilled pattern maker and engineer, whose technical ability helped to keep the cinema going in the war years and in the lean years before closure. He was soon involved in the installation of Western Electric Sound in September, 1929, which resulted in the screening of *The Singing Fool* on 14th October, only a fortnight after Northampton had it. Renamed the County in 1932, the cinema passed to the Odeon circuit around 1941 without any further name change.

It was Rank's early spate of rationalisation of elderly properties which spelled the end for the County, with Mr. Betteridge still manager. The demise of the 46 year-old cinema was marked by a retrospective article in the local press, and an appreciation of Mr. Betteridge's willingness to assist many charitable causes. At 10.18 p.m. precisely on the cinema clock on 29th June, 1957, a few patrons saw the last picture show. It was *Doctor at Large* — remember James Robertson Justice as the irascible surgeon confronting the bungling Dr. Sparrow played by Dirk Bogarde? The demolition of the County did not take place for 15 years, but a photograph in the local press taken in 1972 shows the frontage, minus canopy, looking for all the world like, would you believe, a Methodist chapel.

The Stacey Hill Museum in Wolverton has a 1923 vintage poster advertising a special film show on Monday, 19th June. Held in honour of an old friend, Sam Dawson, 'who had been ill a long time', the film chosen was *Love Maggy*, a story of a chorus girl's marriage into the peerage, starring Peggy Hyland.

BLETCHLEY STUDIO The exterior has less charm than the interior
Photo: Martin Tapsell

The name Studio today often causes one to think of a modern multi-screen complex, but Bletchley's present cinema was thus named right from the beginning. Plans for the new cinema were approved initially in April, 1935, and construction started just over a year later. Built in what was then Bletchley Road (now Queensway), the Studio stands on the Fenny side of a modern covered market in the main shopping street. The opening ceremony took place on 5th October, 1936, performed by Mr. C.D. Flack, J.P., chairman of Bletchley Urban District Council, after which the patrons saw Gary Cooper and Jean Arthur in *Mr. Deeds Goes to Town*. There was evidently a full house, with hundreds waiting outside when the cinema opened its doors at 6.30 p.m. The film was a great draw in itself, having just been transferred straight from the Regal, Marble Arch, where 250,000 people had paid to see it.

The proprietor of this one floor 890 seat cinema was Mr. C. Burnett, but it was not much more than a year or so before the Studio passed into the Shipman & King Circuit. It remained an S. & K. house until that company was merged with ABC (now Thorn EMI) in 1967. The Studio was equipped with RCA sound and Ross projectors. Outside it has rather a squat appearance, having a long single floor auditorium. The seating is divided into four blocks with three aisles. The cinema enthusiast should look out for the carpeting down the aisles, look up to the yellow ceiling, at the red walls and at the contrast band of blue at the join. The stepped trough housing concealed lighting is also very appealing as are the two blancmange shaped decorative features on the ante-proscenium. There are also some original lights at the back of the auditorium. The small foyer is less attractive decoratively, being painted out in pink and purple. There is a central pay box and sales kiosk.

The Studio is opened nightly, with a Saturday matinee. Together with the Electra, Newport Pagnell, the cinema caters for Milton Keynes City residents beyond the old boundaries of Bletchley urban district. Late night shows are included in the programming, plus a number of X certificates that the Electra might prefer not to screen. EMI were reported in the summer of 1982 to be actively considering twinning, presumably by providing back to back auditoria seating about 300 each with a two-way projection box in the middle.

During the last War, Bletchley Park, which had been the home of wealthy businessman, Sir Herbert Leon, became the centre of a vast covert operation to decipher German Intelligence. Some 10,000 people were engaged by the War Office in decoding 'Enigma' and other intelligence traffic, and the Victorian Tudor-Gothic mansion soon became overcrowded. Among the buildings that sprouted in the extensive grounds was the Wilton Hall, an extremely utilitarian red brick structure used for live and film entertainment. After the War, in 1948, the Wilton Hall became Bletchley U.D.C.'s largest hall for many years, being used mainly for dances. In late 1957, the Council were planning to reintroduce films there, following the demise of the County earlier that year (see page 22). However, the management of the Studio cinema opposed any plan to operate a cinema at the expense of the ratepayers, so presumably the proposal was dropped.

BOURNE END

A modern Thames-side resort with a marina and one main shopping street, 2½ miles east north east of Marlow.

Almost last in the queue for a purpose-built cinema, Bourne End waited until 1934. However, there were films in the Abbotsbrook Hall from at least 1920, where an operating box had been constructed outside the building for safety reasons. The Royalty Theatre which appropriately incorporated stage facilities, was the corner piece in a new parade of shops. It opened before the shops, being hurried along by builders Walter Taylor of Harrow in time for New Year's day, 1934. The ceremony was performed by Lieut. Col. W.B. Dupre, J.P. of Wilton Park, Beaconsfield. First films on screen were *I Adore You* which starred Margot Graham, and *Ex Lady* starring Bette Davis. Another early attraction, which Bourne End claimed as a first, was the screen revue *Moonlight Melody* starring the four Eton Boys, the Waldorf Astoria orchestra and fifty

BOURNE END ROYALTY An early 1934 view of the cinema
Photo: Wally Dent

American showgirls. 'You must be early!'counselled the management. Cookham residents had an added inducement to cross the then toll bridge, their 1/- toll fee being refunded on production of a toll ticket at the box office!

Designed by architects Alfred and Vincent Burr, the Royalty was never a pretentious cinema, but it must have looked impressive at night with its mainly red neon name signs. The facade designed by Langley Taylor was drawn together by continuous neon tubing along the whole parade. Inside there was a raked auditorium seating 600, and a small stage used periodically by military bands and artistes until at least the end of the War. There was 3 colour stage lighting, and the screen was the 'largest telescopic size available'. In the first three years there were several proprietors (G.C. Benton, W.E. Walton and Charles F. Cheshir, formerly an estate agent). However, the long reign of Gilbert Church began in 1937. He was a rarity in that he not only owned this one cinema, but he also had a film renting business in Wardour Street and his own film company. He took the Royalty staff up to London to witness the making of his nun-filled movie, *The Angelus*. Perhaps this mollified the Lord's Day Observance Society, who had reported the cinema in its first year for including a film in an advertised Sunday programme!

The best years were in the War, when the blackout restricted movement and a large army camp at Wooburn Green needed entertaining. As with other

BOURNE END ROYALTY Newly appointed staff parade outside in 1934 Left to right; Philip Tickman (page boy), Miss Violet Sabin (usherette), Bobby Townsend, Miss Enid Taylor (usherette), Fred Allen (manager), Miss Florrie Carmichael (usherette), Mr Wally and Mrs Doris Dent (projectionist and cashier)
Photo: Wally Dent

small towns, attendances slumped after television came in the fifties, as few as 12 people putting in an appearance by the summer of 1957, this despite prices below other cinemas at 3/6d and 1/6d. Gilbert Church, who had recently moved to Bognor Regis, decided to close down after showing *The King and I* on 14th December, 1957. Mr. Warner, the manager, did some redecorating and general repairs, and said the cinema would re-open if patrons showed enough interest. They did, and Mr. Gilbert wished to honour his contracts with the distributors, so the Royalty was back in business on 6th January, 1958. But not much longer, as rising costs and the difficulty of pleasing a community of varied tastes led to the final closure on 30th May, 1959. The last film was the western *Jesse James*.

Converted to commercial use, a small cafe was opened in the stage area, the first one to operate in the building. The car park to the rear was sold off for new shops. Today the wood panelled foyer of the furniture discount warehouse is totally shop-like, but the auditorium shell can still be seen, with two attractive glazed light panels with decorated surrounds in the arched ceiling. The proscenium arch is stuffed with giant rolls of carpets, and one projection port is still glazed, serving as an observation window from the upstairs office. A new side balcony houses a selection of divan beds along the right-hand side. Outside the canopy has gone, but in the roof the old ventilation fan still turns idly in the wind.

BOURNE END ROYALTY Mr Wally Dent poses beside his projection
equipment in the Royalty
Photo: Wally Dent

BUCKINGHAM

An historic market town with many Georgian buildings, situated in the
rural north west of the county.

The Electric Cinema began using the larger public room in the Town Hall,
Market Square from about 1916. The proprietors were Messrs. R. & H. Chapman,
whose name is best known now for the old established photographic studios.
The hall seated 340, which later declined to 250. To comply with regulations, a
new fire-proof operating and rewinding room was completed at the end of 1930,
utilising the old surveyor's office adjacent to the main hall.

When the Chandos (see page 28) was built, the Electric was superseded,
closing at the end of 1933 prior to the opening of the new cinema. Buckingham
Town Council agreed to buy 128 seats from the proprietor at a cost of 4/6d
each, or £28 16s. for the whole consignment, which presumably were retained in
the Town Hall for use in other entertainments and functions.

The uniquely named Chandos cinema was built on a corner site in what is
now London Road, but was then Chandos Road, after the Dukes of Buckingham

BUCKINGHAM CHANDOS The uniquely named Chandos on 10th July 1982
Photo: Martin Tapsell

and Chandos. Plans for the cinema were submitted by Satchwell and Roberts to the Town Council in 1933, and were passed to the county branch of the Council for the Preservation of Rural England for comment. The Town Council approved the plans, but resolved on 4th September, 1933 that the roof be apple green, following the CPRE's recommendation for a rural cinema. For some unexplained reason, the tiles in question, which appear original, are red!

A distinguished gathering were present on 29th January, 1934, including the Mayor, Lord Addington, to witness the opening ceremony performed by Lady Bowyer. There was no time for a trial run of the talking apparatus, as the proprietor, Walter Parker and his staff were working on it almost to the eleventh hour. The local press and the speakers at the ceremony were highly complimentary on this "gem of artistry". Mr. Parker, who was to become a popular councillor, was praised for his distinctive and romantic enterprise. This small brick-built cinema looks towards the town centre, its auditorium at a slight angle to the frontage, resulting in a wedge-shaped foyer. Originally seating 450, the construction was very much a local affair, the architect, Mr. Roberts being at school with the builder, C.T. Cecil. The auditorium had delicate green walls, with a shell pink stage setting. At the beginning there were nightly performances, two on Mondays, Thursdays and Saturdays supplemented by a children's matinee on Saturdays at 2.30 p.m.

Buckingham provides an interesting example on how quickly the cinema industry could respond to a crisis in pre-war days. The talking apparatus being unsatisfactory, a representative of BTP sound called on Tuesday evening. He sent for a more senior executive, who arrived at 1 a.m. on Wednesday, spending 3 hours inspecting the auditorium and preparing a contract. The principal and departmental heads were summoned from their beds, as were engineers and technicians from all over London. The equipment was drawn from stores, and rushed to Buckingham by fast lorry that same Wednesday, to be installed for use at 5.30, just 30 minutes before the contract deadline. Normally the period from contract to completion of installation would have been 10 days, so the Chandos must have been something of a record.

The cinema remained independent, the present proprietor, K.G. Randall taking over from Mrs. Gwen Harris in 1968. Mrs. Harris, who lives nearby, retains an active interest in the Chandos, relieving the present manager, Robert Tear during his holidays. The proprietor has another slightly smaller cinema in St. Ives, Cambridgeshire, which is separately managed. One curious feature of the Chandos is its stained glass windows, which unless they were curtained, must have let in some light during daylight hours. The new owner had these blacked over, but a problem still arises from the level access to the stalls, as daylight through the foyer can filter through to the screen when patrons enter. 1968 saw the introduction of the present two-day bingo policy on Mondays and Fridays, but apart from one scoreboard in the auditorium, film-goers do not see much difference. Two gaming machines are brought out of a store room on club nights. Today's respaced seating capacity is down to 380, with 68 seats in the small balcony directly over the foyer. Interestingly, some original green studded seats of the armless variety survive in the front stalls. The screen is literally silver (coated), whereas most now have a matt surface. The present decor is red ceiling and walls, with a blue lower band and proscenium arch, and yellow radiators.

The Chandos has benefited marginally from the coming of the independent University College at Buckingham. In its early years a film club using the cinema was founded by the students, who were admitted at a reduced price to special screenings once a month. For example, *The Great Gatsby* was shown on 26th July, 1978 and *Fellini Satyricon* a month later (Students 70p and 75p). However, as the UCB courses are intensive and the students more mobile, they have not established the same presence as can be experienced in say, Oxbridge cinemas. Occasional live shows are held on the small stage, those aiming at a family audience being most successful — a special appearance by David Kossoff being a typical example.

BURNHAM

A large residential village, 4 miles east of Slough, Berks.

Burnham in 1915 would have been quite a small village, and was thus quite privileged to possess the Burnham Electric Theatre from at least that date. The cinema almost escaped a mention in the trade directories, but we do know the proprietor for most of its life was Mr. C.H. Jarratt who also owned a hardware store where the National Westminster Bank now stands. The brick-built Electric still stands about 50 yards from the High Street in Lincoln Hatch Lane. Patrons entered down a side passageway, paying as little as one penny to see the golden silent stars like Pearl White, Charlie Chaplin, the Keystone Cops and poker-faced Buster Keaton. The admission price was paid to Dolly Strong (later to be Dolly Watson), the film was projected by Cyril Cox (an ardent Chelsea supporter in his spare time) and piano accompaniment was provided by Gertie Murkett.

The Electric was not the perfect picture house — film breakdowns, which were commonplace, were greeted by a great stamping of hob-nailed boots on the wooden floor. Mr. Jarratt would pick on some juvenile miscreant, and eject him down the wooden steps from the back door. In between such strenuous acts the proprietor would also disinfect the audience and vend sweets and soft drinks, stacking the empties under a seat beside the piano. It was a favourite prank to upset these bottles whilst being ejected for causing a disturbance — today's youths continue the tradition by stamping on their plastic Kiora cartons!

It seems the Electric had brushes with the General Purposes Committee over its sanitary arrangements, or lack of them. There were no toilets, resulting in unfortunate activity outside the building. Our best information is that films ceased around 1931 without ever going over to sound. The Electric continued briefly as a live theatre, although inevitably the actors were mostly approaching retirement. Subsequently the building became Balm's furniture depository (later Savages) and latterly an engineering works. Just a few Burnhamites recall its days as a centre of entertainment but many probably are unaware that Burnham ever had a cinema.

CHALFONT ST. PETER

A large, not particularly historic looking village, just off the A 413. Gold Hill with its common, adjoins.

The Memorial Hall in the Broadway was opened by Admiral Lord Beatty in 1920, in memory of the fallen in the Great War. One resident recalls that there were two halls standing side by side, which had been procured as Army surplus buildings and were formerly standing in Denham. The usual whist drives, dances and social functions were held, but in 1930, the hut furthest from the main road became the Broadway Cinema. The 400 seat cinema was intended to help pay off the overdraft on the buildings with the receipts from the thrice weekly film shows. Although there may have been some rake to the floor, it was not sufficient for rear projection so back projection was used.

The Broadway management were alarmed in 1937 by the proposal of Charles Cheshir to build an entirely new cinema in the village. Only by pleading possible insolvency were the objectors able to persuade the Bucks CC General Purposes Committee to reject the application. At this time the cinema was operated by Messrs. Weller and Stevenson, whose mini circuit also included the Carlton, Princes Risborough and the Picture House, Beaconsfield. In 1943, Sunday entertainment was allowed for the first time, but for H.M. forces and their paying guests only. Films finally ceased on or about the 31st December, 1951, after which the hall was put up for sale. Its eventual fate was demolition in 1962, and today the site near the Market Place is occupied by modern shops.

The Gold Hill Cinema, or Palace, recedes even further into the mists of time, but apparently showed films between c. 1914-30. First advertised as the Palace in November, 1914. Drama, comedy, cowboy, travel interest and war pictures would be shown. Admission was 3d and 6d, nightly from 6.30 — 10.30. Bicycles and prams were stored free. "Sid Hill's" was situated in Grove Lane in what then must have been a semi-rural locality. The original premises were somewhat rough and ready — probably an accommodation building procured secondhand from railway works carried out at Gerrards Cross. The proprietor, Sidney Herbert Hill worked as a journeyman painter, but was careful to inform his workmates what fine entertainment he provided. His orchestra consisted of a pianist, Elsie Adams, who was virtually stone deaf, but claimed reassuringly that she could hear her piano when wearing her pince-nez glasses!

In the mid twenties, Mr. Hill replaced his original premises with a utilitarian barn-like building. Around 1930 when the Broadway opened, film performances ceased and the hall turned to dancing and skating instead. When Mr. Hill died around 1935, his widow Louisa Agnes took over the licence. In the Second World War, like many smaller cinemas, it was used for storing furniture made homeless by the blitz. At some stage after the War, the building became known as the Old Rink Printing Works, and is currently used by the printers K. Vine. Today, the former Palace looks rather like a village hall, except for a taller brick elevation facing Grove Lane which would have housed the foyer and projection room. It is strange to reflect that this former cinema, which even cinema enthusiasts have hardly heard of, was in 1915, one of only two cinemas advertised in the local press covering a wide area of South Bucks, Middlesex and North London — the other one was the Notting Hill Coronet.

Whilst in the neighbourhood, it is not without interest that the headquarters of Services Sound and Vision Corporation (known until 1982 as Services Kinema Corporation) are situated at the end of Chalfont Grove off Narcot Lane. This wooded rural situation conceals the focal point of a chain of some nine far-flung cinemas, not least of which is our own Astra at R.A.F. Halton Camp.

CHESHAM

A lengthy town on the River Chess. A spur of the Metropolitan line ends here, but the river flows straight on, as does a considerable volume of through traffic.

The first building to show films over a long period was the Town Hall, where "pictures" were screened from 1907. Not much detail was given at first, although press advertising assured the public that they were "the finest possible to see" and apparently included a lot of wild west films. After a gap, the films began again in February, 1912, on a regular once nightly basis, with three performances on Saturdays, at prices from 1d to 2d and 3d. One report of much later date states that one chairman of the Urban District Council had in younger days, played here on the piano, accompanying silent pictures. It is not certain when exactly films ceased, but by the First World War, Chesham had two cinemas designed for the purpose.

Much later in 1962, the Town Hall was damaged by an arsonist, having been already abandoned by the Town Council some years earlier. It was in fact being used for commercial storage, but after considerable heart-searching about its architectural merits, the decaying building in the town centre was finally demolished in February, 1965.

The Empire Cinema stood at the upper end of Station Road, not far from the station. It opened on 4th July, 1912 with a benefit performance on behalf of Chesham Cottage Hospital. The film chosen was a fine animal picture by the Selig Company called *Saved by her Lion*. In those early days, the star was unrecorded in the press. The hall measured 60 x 40 feet and the three proprietors were Messrs. Walter Charles Wilson, Wicks and Gabriel. They had come to Chesham in search of an opportunity to provide a purpose-built cinema where none existed. Previously in Tonbridge, the proprietors were no doubt relieved that the Empire stood on rising ground, the Star Cinema at Tonbridge having suffered regular flooding from the nearby river! The Empire was erected by builders Rust and Ratcliffe and constructed in expanded steel with concrete walls. The resulting fire resistance and the provision of six exits was much stressed in the press advertising for 'the family resort'. There were 400 tip-up seats and electric lighting installed by R.J.J. Swan, manager of the local electric light company.

A separate box housed the Kamm bioscope machine, which had fire-proof asbestos walls. Apart from films, concerts were also held whilst the pianist at film performances was Henry Rose. One memorable variety act to play the Empire was Lady Little, who came in September, 1914. She was billed as the world's tiniest woman — only 25 inches high, weighing 14¾ lbs and aged 21 years 9 months. Not surprisingly she had enjoyed a "meteoric success in five continents" with the curious public. Despite such attractions however, the Empire had a fairly short career as an entertainment venue, having closed as such by 1920. It reappears in directories as the Empire Poster Works, but was used for the billeting of troops during the Second World War and was subsequently demolished.

The Palace, later renamed the Astoria, now stands empty in the Broadway only a few yards from the bottom of Station Road. The first press advertising for the cinema appears for the Gaumont drama *Neath the Lion's Paw* showing from 26th June, 1914, which, if the cinema's first film, gives an interesting comparison with the Empire. Built by Clark's of Watford, the proprietor was again Mr. Walter Charles Wilson, who later leased the cinema out after it became the Astoria in 1930. The cinema had a stage 14 feet deep, two dressing rooms and a balcony. In 1914 it cost 2d, 3d, 4d, 6d or 1/- to enter, presumably with a

CHESHAM ASTORIA Taken during the 1950's
Photos: Kevin Wheelan

reduction for children at the Saturday matinees. One particularly interesting film, which Mr. Wilson arranged to be taken, was of a Chesham v Slough football match. Held on Saturday, 4th November, 1922, the plan was to show it in Chesham first if the home team won, or Slough if they did not. In the event, Chesham ran the Slough defenders to a standstill, and the opposing team went down to a 5—1 defeat!

By 1938, the Astoria was managed by Shipman & King, who were the final proprietors when it was decided that Chesham did not need two cinemas in the same circuit. That decision was made in 1959, and the 505 seat cinema went dark on 23rd May, 1959. The last films shown were *Never Steal Anything Small* and *No Name on the Bullet* starring likeable western hero, Audie Murphy. For many years the Astoria was the home of a furnishing store owned by the London Co-operative Society, but they vacated the premises around the end of 1981. The present plate glass frontage right up to the gable is vaguely suggestive of a new church on a housing estate, but no activity, either secular or ecclesiastical was taking place at the time of writing.

The late lamented Embassy, Germain Street is sadly missed by cinema enthusiasts, who relished the thirties ambience it retained until the end. Designed by David Evelyn Nye, it was one of several for the rising Shipman & King Circuit, other cinemas Nye undertook including the Embassys at Petts Wood and Esher. All were carefully tailored to fit in with their surroundings and

33

CHESHAM EMBASSY
Photos: Kevin Wheelan

this, in 1937, was one of 20 S. & K. cinemas, the nearest being the Rex at Berkhamsted (still open). The opening day had been awaited with great interest locally, especially as the construction by Bovis had featured the removal from the railway station of a giant girder which took a whole day. The ceremony on 11th January, 1937 was to have been performed by Lord Chesham, M.C., J.P., but as he was indisposed, the chairman of the U.D.C., Mr. E. Culverhouse, took his place. As at the Odeon, Aylesbury, a Shirley Temple film was booked for the first week, this time being *Poor Little Rich Girl*. The actor, John Lodge, was also at the opening, rushing straight from Elstree after making *Bulldog Drummond*. He was still in make up, but as he observed, this was better than no appearance at all.

The frontage of the Embassy used local facing bricks, and incorporated shops on either side of the entrance. Inside, the foyer had two curved staircases leading invitingly to the cafe and circle. The cafe, with its glass partition was much admired in architectural journals. Until the end, one half of the cafe retained its original Shipman & King carpet, although in the last few months, it was somewhat obscured by the vast quantity of secondhand books being sold there. As to the auditorium itself, perhaps the most distinctive feature was the acoustic panels each side of the proscenium, which were in the form of square panels (blue) from which gilded protuberances somewhat reminiscent of giant collar studs could be seen. There was provision made for an organ which was never installed. Seating capacity at the outset was 1,146 which fell slightly to 1,098 by 1981.

A feature of this off main street cinema which I particularly liked was the extensive use of neon. Green continuous tubing was used to draw the whole frontage (shops and cinema) together, and there was a striking vertical Embassy name sign in red neon, with contrast tubing in green. The sign failed only months before the closure. As late as 1980, the future seemed bright with tripling being on the cards for the only cinema in the Chiltern District area. In January, manager Richard Wright was pictured in the press beside £20,000 worth of new projection equipment, which had replaced the original installation including xenon arcs. Mr. Wright invited any genuinely interested members of the public to witness the installation of the new equipment.

Despite this expenditure, attendances became increasingly disappointing to Thorn-EMI who were the recipients of a petition with 3,275 signatures after a decision to close had been made. The 17 employees at the Embassy (including Jessica Bone who had been cleaning there ever since 1937) were quoted in the press as favouring more children's films, ethnic shows and greater publicity as the salvation of the cinema. In the end however, Thorn-EMI were not to be moved from their position that Chesham was no longer viable. Chesham people evidently had some affection for the building, as a full house said their farewells on 24th April, 1982 at the last screening of *Evil Under the Sun*. Fortunately, the Museum of London were made fully aware of the closure, and many photographs were taken for their archive. The Museum also acquired (as accession 82-300) a sampling of seats, lights and carpeting. About 30 more seats found their way to Buckingham to furnish a mini cinema in the new Home Movie Museum.

The Embassy was demolished in June 1983.

FARNHAM COMMON

A later offshoot of Farnham Royal, situated between Slough and Beaconsfield.

There was a cinema in Farnham Common from the very early date (for a village) of March, 1914. The Cinema had been built on vacant land in the Broadway during the previous year, its first proprietor being a Mr. Herbert Dowsing, whom some informants tell me was a German. The Cinema, or Plaza as it came to be known, was basically a public hall with a stage, dressing rooms, a smaller hall and kitchen. As a cinema it held 350, later reduced to 210 by 1939. In the early days the operator, Cyril Spuffard was always having trouble with the electric engine at the back breaking down. Other personalities still remembered by long term residents of the village were Mr. Yates, who brought chocolates and sweets over from his parents' sweet shop opposite, and Mr. Wheeler, who played a wind-up gramophone before there was a piano. Serials were the order of the day, one being *The Seven Pearls* in which a Turkish detective recovered a Sultan's stolen pearls over seven episodes.

The hall doubled as a sale room for the Red Cross in aid of the troops in the First World War. There were a succession of proprietors, including H.B. Pallett of Slough who received a licence in 1926 subject to some wooden cupboards under the stairs being bricked up. More alterations had to be made in 1930 before the General Purposes Committee would re-licence the cinema.

FARNHAM COMMON CINEMA
Photo: Kevin Wheelan

Films ceased altogether between 1933 and 1938, when Mr. Van Biene took over. Further name changes took place, the cinema being called the Beeches in 1939, then the Beacon. For the greater part of the Second World War, the building was used as a canteen, then becoming dilapidated, was renovated and used for general purposes including whist drives, receptions, concerts, bridge clubs and British Legion meetings. The last brief period as a cinema came after the Second World War under the proprietorship of Myles Byrne, who named the cinema the Curzon. However, in September of that year, there was a planning application for conversion into a furniture depository but a local history of the district states that the Beacon Press acquired the building as a printing works. This early cinema still stands today, sharing the fate of its contemporary, the Gold Hill Cinema, remaining a printing works trading as the Capital Press.

GERRARDS CROSS

A leafy residential town on the Banbury-Marylebone commuter line, and developed mainly in the inter-war years.

The highly successful Classic cinema originally opened as the Playhouse on 12th October, 1925. Richard Denny starred in *I'll Show You the Town* with live support from Dominico Pacitti on his famous Carlo Bergonzi violin. The most

37

GERRARDS CROSS PLAYHOUSE
Photos: Kevin Wheelan

distinctive architectural feature remains the octagonal tower, which serves as a corner piece. The tower once had three arched entrances with Georgian style doors, but these have now been replaced by plate glass at ground floor level. Inside the tower, the pay box stood to the left, as it does today, although further from the entrance doors. Intriguingly, the 1947 local guide refers to the Playhouse as modelled on the one adjoining Buckingham Palace — perhaps the Grecian pillars along the left-hand side of the old auditorium did have a regal look!

The first proprietor was the ubiquitous Charles F. Cheshir, with Eric Cheshir as manager. In his day, prices of admission were 8d, 1/3d, 1/10d and 2/4d, all to the single floor auditorium. There were also boxes at the rear seating four persons and costing 12/6d apiece. There was a stage, orchestra pit, also dressing rooms to the right of the 25 feet wide proscenium arch. Both a cafe and a dance hall were also provided. Before the Second World War, Gerrards Cross Operatic Society performed here on stage, whilst 567 people could be accommodated for films. Films changed three times a week, with a Saturday morning children's club.

In June, 1950, several alterations were approved. They involved blocking the rear exits to Elthorpe Crescent, erecting a large continuous poster board to draw attention to the off main street cinema, removing the boxes and taking out some rear stalls, repositioning the barrier behind them. The raking of the auditorium floor was also improved. There were several changes of ownership until the cinema passed from Southan Morris to Essoldo in or about 1962. Essoldo, then an expanding cinema circuit, retained the name Playhouse until November, 1969. The justification for re-naming the cinema Essoldo was the major facelift which had taken place over the previous two months. The auditorium was re-painted black with matching newly designed tip-up seats (392 in total). These seats were developed by Essoldo Furnishers (Glasgow) Ltd., being of the new 'Esquire' single pedestal style with individual arm-rests. These were first installed in Gerrards Cross. For colour contrast, red carpeting and wall curtaining was provided. The former cold discomfort was also dissipated by new oil-fired heating and new air conditioning. The opening film in the re-styled Essoldo was a gala charity performance of *Battle of Britain* with guest of honour, Air Marshal Clayton, Chief of Staff, R.A.F. Strike Command on 29th November, 1969.

As Essoldo, like Granada, turned increasingly to bingo, the Classic chain acquired the Essoldo, changing its name to Classic from the first showing of *Paint Your Wagon* on 26th March, 1972. Classic soon formulated plans to build an extra auditorium seating 304, but this was refused in 1973 on environmental and car parking grounds. So was a second attempt in 1978 for a more modest 140 seat mini auditorium. The final solution was an internal reconstruction by which a second auditorium was built over the rear stalls. Screen Two faces the opposite way from Screen One below, with the projection box being re-sited in the middle of the roof, with projection in both directions from different levels. Today, the foyer is deeper, and immediately inside the tower there is a sales kiosk, which also has a hatch opening to Screen One. The twins opened for business on 22nd September, 1979 and seat 368 and 213 respectively, thus increasing the former total.

The lower auditorium is more satisfactory in that patrons enter from the rear rather than from the side, and Screen Two patrons were experiencing some noisy ventilation during my mid-Summer visit. However, patrons were all admitted at a standard time, thus avoiding the need to wait for their screen to open. On a warm Sunday in July, it was notable that the 30 space car park was already full to overflowing by 5 p.m. Patrons in this commuter zone are discerning, and quality films are well received.

HALTON CAMP ASTRA taken in July 1980
Photo: Martin Tapsell

HALTON CAMP, Near Wendover

An R.A.F. training establishment in a very pleasant setting on the edge of wooded Chiltern countryside. A former Rothschild mansion serves as the officers' mess.

There have been Astra cinemas in many far flung parts of the globe — R.A.F. Kabrit in the Egyptian canal zone, R.A.F. Habbaniya, Iraq and R.A.F. Sharjah in the Gulf to name but three. Our local Astra is one of only four left in the U.K., so something of a rarity. The present building dates back to 1925, so has been a familiar sight to apprentices almost from the very first years of the base. This Astra is no nissen hut, but a free-standing, brick-built cinema, standing well back from the Wendover-Tring road. It was licenced in January, 1926, despite the fact that the Air Council believed that the 1909 Act did not bind the crown. The licence was renewed each year until 1932 when a new Army and Air Force Act specifically excluded service cinemas. The Astra holds 589 inclusive of the balcony which was used initially by officers and their friends only. So popular was the entertainment that junior ranks were sometimes told to stand down in their favour when queues grew too long.

The Astra had, and to a certain extent retains, a personality of its own. The audiences react positively to films, supplementing the dialogue with the odd wisecrack, cheering as the lights dim and booing the D. Bennett advertising. The over mushy or sentimental films were thought to be fair game for some regular hecklers who vied with each other to keep the audience in cahoots of laughter for as long as possible! Heaven help those actors posing as macho all Americans on the screen who were known to be "chicken" in real life. Should a film break or lose alignment on the screen, the projectionist can expect to be "made aware of the event" by a chorus of catcalls, whistles and stamping rising from the floor below. The crush to gain admission by junior ranks caused the positioning of service policemen inside the doors each side of the stage, which were once used as additional entrances. A charge ensued as soon as the lock bars were heard to click open, and the S.P.'s fervently wished they were back in their guardroom! The hapless S.P.'s were often "accidentally" knocked backwards up the two steps inside the doors! However, in 1947, a particularly boisterous incursion resulted in a apprentice falling in the crush. Apparently unhurt, he took his seat, but died during the performance from a crushed rib-cage. This served to calm things down considerably from then on.

Resuming our history, we note that the cinema suffered a rare misfortune (for Bucks anyway) of having a fire in the projection room. However, the fire (in June, 1930) was soon put out and everyone safely evacuated. Sunday film shows were allowed much earlier than elsewhere in view of the large number of 15-17 year olds in the camp at weekends — doubtless leave was not so forthcoming before the last war. When this broke out, a large hut became known as the "No. 2 Wing cinema" serving as an overflow to the main cinema during the evenings. 16 mm. wartime and pre-war films were screened plus cartoons. Usually these hutted cinemas were used during the day time to show aircraft recognition and training films. Most folded soon after peace was declared and became social clubs or hobby centres for aero-modelling and the like. Halton's ceased showing films around 1947. At this time apprentices were earning 10/- per fortnight, or £1 per fortnight after attaining the age of 17½, so that the Astra's cheapest seats, at 3d, were much sought after!

In the post-war period, the Astra was run by the R.A.F. Cinema Corporation, which became the Services Kinema Corporation after merging with the Army circuit in 1969, and in mid 1982, the Services Sound and Vision Corporation. The SSVC headquarters are near Chalfont St. Peter (q.v.). Their Bucks cinema is faced in roughcast with the name Astra on an illuminated sign over the canopy. The foyer contains a pay box to the left, where admission at £1.20 per head is excellent value these days. Directly ahead, patrons can spend a bit more at the "Candy bar". Pausing to pick up a monthly programme, and glance at the posters over the entrance doors, the patron takes the left one of two doors to the stalls. The balcony is now closed, but until 1981 it was possible to sit up there for the same price (then 90p). The auditorium is a fair size by today's standards. The walls are Air Force blue, with beige and cream pilasters and a curved and banded ceiling. These bands are ornamented in some fine detail, as are the headboards over the exit doors — proof of the craftsmanship of the apprentices who worked on the cinema. There are bare boards under the red tip-up seats, but linoleum down the side and centre aisles. Airmen are asked by a notice in the foyer not to rest their feet on the row in front, which they don't very often, although one winter night was so cold that several chose to perch on the radiator pipes!

Upstairs is a spacious cloakroom and the manager's office, at present occupied by Mr. T. Bailey. A door marked 'gents' also takes you to the projection room until recently Eric's domain. One unusual feature of this cinema is that there is a clock at the back of the stalls, but it is not electric, so its ticking can be heard in quiet moments by the audience. SSVC try not to have too much of these quiet moments, as the airmen prefer action, comedy and let's face it, a little vigorous sex. In a typical week all three can be provided as there are three programme changes per week. The cinema is open nightly, except Mondays and Tuesdays, for service personnel and their families. Programmes change on Sundays, Thursdays and Saturdays when an X is likely. The late Mary Millington used to draw some very good houses, so one hopes the industry will find a worthy successor! There is not much censorship now, but I'm told that during 1952-53 the film *Quo Vadis* was banned from R.A.F. cinemas the world over. If it was thought to be subversive of military discipline, one wonders what they would have made of *Stripes* which today's apprentices have enjoyed? The video boom seems to have taken a toll of Astra audiences in the last year and at the end of August 1983, the cinema closed when the Air Force decided to run the cinema, taking over from Services Sound and Vision Corporation. Prolonged negotiations about the handover then began, but the cinema was still closed over a month later.

SSVC manager Mr. Bailey and the cashier would not be staying on, and a serviceman was to be appointed manager.

HIGH WYCOMBE

Until recently, the largest town in Bucks, in which the largest undivided cinema in the county still continues, although its days are numbered. The firm of Pixton, who occupied their Queens Road factory in October, 1925, were one of nearly 50 firms supplying seating to cinemas in the golden era.

In view of its status, it is not surprising to learn that Wycombe was first to obtain a building specifically intended to exhibit films. The Picture Palace or

HIGH WYCOMBE PALACE High Wycombe's first Palace, showing its ecclesiastical origins.
Photo: Ron Goodearl

Palace in Frogmore was, however, a conversion. Originally a Primitive Methodist chapel, it had been a Salvation Army citadel and barracks for 25 years until they moved to new premises. Mr. H. Leslie Bell acquired the property in 1909, redecorating the interior, providing electric lighting and new doors, which opened outwards as required by the Borough Council. Animated pictures, illustrated songs, high-class vaudeville and "specialities" were offered twice nightly at 7 and 9 p.m. plus Saturday matinees at 2.30 p.m. The first film on 13th September, 1909 was not inappropriately *The Salvation Army Lass* — 'a beautiful picture of great human interest'. To retain the religious connection, charitable sacred concerts were held on Sundays.

Although it was too early to show actual newsreels, there was an arrangement with *Lloyds News* and the *Daily Chronicle* that any news that was too late for inclusion in the press could be displayed on a white sheet at the Palace on receipt of a telegram. It is unclear whether the Palace ever received a licence, as the County's General Purposes Committee complained to Chepping Wycombe Town Clerk that the cinema had opened without one. Outside, the Palace appears from photographs very little altered from chapel days. Next door there was a skating rink in which there is evidence that films were also shown. In fact skating rinks were among the first halls used as makeshift cinemas before the 1909 act.

43

The short lived Palace was seriously damaged by fire on Sunday, 9th June, 1912. £900 worth of damage was sustained including the loss of scenery for the Cinderella pantomime, although 7,000 feet of film survived in a fire-proof enclosure, as did the neighbouring Parker's furniture factory. Neither the proprietor Leslie Bell, (who was ill at the time), nor his manager W.T. Winepress could have been much consoled by the advert placed immediately under the report of the fire in the *Bucks Free Press*. Under the slogan 'Your Palace needs protection' West Wycombe insurance agent W. Burch advertised his services. The present Palace cinema, which stands opposite its forerunner, can hardly be termed a replacement building, opening as it did over 10 years later.

It was fortunate that by the time the Palace was put out of business, Wycombe had acquired another cinema — the purpose-built Electroscope in Oxford Street. This was opened in style on Wednesday, 28th February, 1912 by Councillor T. Graefe using a solid gold key. A charitable show was held with music from Sims Vaudeville orchestra. The proceeds (£36. 10s. 2d.) went to the cottage hospital.

The Electroscope, which was noted for its eye-catching and sometimes amusing advertising in the local press, was a typical example of early kinema architecture. The entrance to the cinema was up a passageway with a butcher's

HIGH WYCOMBE ELECTROSCOPE A pre-1930 view of the Electroscope in its original state.
Photo: Ron Goodearl

shop to the right. The frontage was richly ornamented with niches for three statues and hanging gas lamps set high on the facade. Seating 750, later reduced to 566, the Electroscope survived until 1930, by which time it had been superseded by more modern cinemas. As we shall see, it was to rise again, but meantime we leave it derelict and shuttered as we turn our attention to West Wycombe.

HIGH WYCOMBE GRAND seen in better days, c1919
Photo: Ron Goodearl

The Grand cinema, 260 Desborough Road, can be described as suburban, being about a mile from the town centre. It was opened without ceremony on 28th April, 1913 with the film *Zigomar* in which the King of criminals was pitted against Broguet, King of detectives. The 590 seat Grand had the then novel attraction of continuous performances between 6.30 and 10.30 p.m. Admission cost 9d, 6d or 3d, — 1/- for a seat reservation. Patrons were reminded at intervals of the time, which was flashed on the screen instead of the later practice of providing an illuminated clock.

The Grand was built by Gibsons, the High Wycombe builders, and designed by T. Thurlow. The proprietor was C.A. Gibson and the cinema was

45

managed by Edgar Sinclair. The *Bucks Free Press* found it to be one of the finest and cosiest halls in the county. The raked floor, tip-up seating, thick cork carpet, 5 exits, stage and dressing rooms earned the term "palatial" in 1913. A pianist and a string orchestra accompanied the silent films. Being built before the days of mass car ownership, free bicycle storage was advertised in an adjacent garage (at owner's risk).

The Wycombe cinema, as it was frequently referred to in the press, flourished and spent lavishly on advertising. For example when *Daddy Longlegs* starring Mary Pickford was coming to the Grand, announcements were inserted all over the paper — even under motor cycles for sale — just in case any film goer overlooked the event. From 1929, the Grand was part of a small chain, British Cinematograph Theatres, who had 3 other cinemas, two in Ipswich, one in Southampton. After the War, business remained good for a time, the Grand being the first cinema in town to get Cinemascope. However, the decline in admissions in the fifties hit suburban cinemas the hardest, and by then the epithet Grand was no longer entirely appropriate to the struggling cinema. In 1953, the cinema closed for several months until purchased by Atkinson & Rees Ltd., of the Kingsway Cinema, Mile Hill, Bristol. The last proprietor, H.C. Orr decided to sell the cinema for retail use in 1962. On Saturday, 8th September, 1962 the late Kenneth More was seen coping with teddy boys in *Some People* with the Edgar Wallace thriller, *Time to Remember* in support. Thereafter part of the cinema was demolished and a service yard provided for the use of the new occupiers, a firm of credit tailors. In more recent years the cinema has been the home of furniture retailers, John Blundell Ltd. and quite recently a new addition to the chain of Ford's discount gas and electrical stores. There is little to see today, as the former frontage has been drastically modernised and the interior re-ceilinged. The neighbourhood is one of mixed industry, residential streets and vacant lots. Next door is still a grocers, but during my visit was selling cards for the Moslem Eid. This leads me to speculate whether the Grand, had it survived a little longer as a cinema, might not have become an Asian language cinema in common with many elsewhere.

For 13 years, the town's only cinema has been the Palace, Frogmore, which opened opposite its short-lived predecessor of that name, on 2nd December, 1922. The architect Gilbert Booth had a difficult site owing to the irregular plan of adjacent buildings. The original front elevation was rendered to resemble a 16th century half-timbered house — a device quite commonly used at that period in appropriate architectural areas. There was a panelled foyer leading to an auditorium, end on to the street. This had a renaissance interior designed by De Jong & Co. with large oil paintings to provide colour. The builders were Hinkins and Frewin of Oxford. It is recorded that the seats were made locally — Wycombe being then as it is now, a chair-making town. Stairs to the left of the foyer approached both the balcony and more immediately the olde worlde tea rooms, later designated the cafe. The Palace was then smaller than today, seating 930 in the stalls and 296 in the balcony (total 1226) but then as now, the proprietors were High Wycombe Theatre Company.

In 1938, the auditorium had been extended bringing the capacity up to

HIGH WYCOMBE PALACE The brightly painted exterior of the town's last cinema in August 1982. The Palace closed very suddenly on Wednesday 21st September 1983 with *Psycho II*.
Photo: Martin Tapsell

HIGH WYCOMBE PALACE when newly extended and modernised in 1938
Photo: Cyril Roberts (Photographer), High Wycombe

1,650 — 150 more than the present total. The Tudor frontage was also replaced by the present plainer elevation which has been painted an eye-catching ocher colour quite recently. The cafe closed around 1963 but is still in use as a dance hall, in which ballroom, Latin-American and disco dancing are taught. Today the interior is still very attractive, the long auditorium being flanked by vertical fins from which recessed orange tinted lighting provides the main illumination. Overhead, the ceiling glows a peach hue during the intervals. For one now accustomed to multi auditoria, 31 rows of stalls seats seems spacious, and no doubt costly to heat in winter. Faced with either subdividing (it being almost impossible to make a single auditorium of any size viable these days) or selling the property, the company opted for the latter course. It must be admitted that some rowdy elements in the audiences have done nothing to help attendances, and one is reminded of these unwelcome trouble makers by the notice in the foyer referring to the bringing in of intoxicating liquor, cooked takeaways, etc., and the summoning of the police to disturbances. Sad when you read in the programme that admission to this rather nice cinema is the lowest in Bucks — at £1.70 in the circle or £1.50 in the stalls. There are special one-day programmes on Sundays, special Saturday matinees in school holidays, and ethnic films for Asians on Sunday afternoons.

Closure of the Palace took place on 22nd September, 1983. John Travolta fans expecting to see the advertised *Staying Alive* film on Thursday were confronted by locked doors and a closed notice.

HIGH WYCOMBE MAJESTIC Showing the exterior (above) and the atmospheric auditorium (opposite).
Photos: High Wycombe Library

By far the grandest cinema ever to be seen in Bucks, and worthy of our cover, was the Majestic in Castle Street. The cinema was opened by the Majestic Theatre Co. on 21st January, 1930, and had 1,486 seats. It was built on a sloping site descending 20 feet towards the High Street, on land provided by H.J. Cox of High Wycombe. 200 local men began working on its construction on 16th July, 1929. The architect, S.B. Pritlove, had designed a similar Majestic in

48

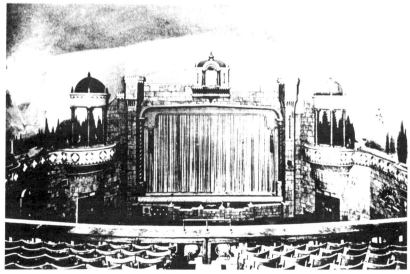

HIGH WYCOMBE MAJESTIC Which became the Odeon.   These views show the remarkable atmospheric auditorium.
Photos: High Wycombe Library

Staines, no more alas. The High Wycombe Majestic undoubtedly can be classified as "atmospheric", inside if not outside. The chairman of the Majestic Theatre Co.'s directors, W.E. Greenwood turned his creative mind to everything from the fibrous plaster ceiling to the usherettes' uniforms. The style of the cinema was Venetian and the walls were hidden by salients covered in towers, turrets and ornamentation. There was a night sky ceiling rather like the one provided at the New Victoria, Edinburgh, seven months earlier. The entrance was flanked by shops, and inside the doors there was a crush hall decorated by fluted columns and arched beams in metallic colours. There was also a very elegant tea lounge and cafe designed to represent a courtyard scene.

The opening was performed by Major General Sir Alfred Knox, M.P. for South Bucks, before an invited audience. Sir Alfred strongly opposed the importation of American films because of the spread of Amercianisms into the English language. However, when he raised the matter in the House, the then government declined to impose direct restrictions on U.S. film imports. The first film shown was *Careers* starring Billy Dove, with Mickey Mouse and a Gaumont British news in support. To supplement the film fare, the Majestic had a Compton organ, a stage and orchestra pit, the stage being 36½ feet wide. The above mentioned cafe was open daily from 11 a.m. until 10.30 p.m. for morning coffee, luncheons, tea and light refreshments. A tea dance was held every Wednesday and Saturday from 4-6 p.m. followed by a special dance on Saturday evening between 8.30 and 10.30 p.m. for which patrons paid 1/-. If they preferred to see a film, they were charged between 8d and 2/4d or 6d, 1/- or 1/6d at matinees, with free car parking. Manager Charles Longman must have been very proud of his establishment.

Talking of establishments, a detailed record of who worked at the Odeon as it was to become, is given in the Odeon Theatres house magazine, *Circle*, May, 1948 issue. A photograph is included showing 24 of the employees, including usherettes and projection staff. The former consisted of Messrs. B. Porter (chief), F. Reed (co-chief), E. Nicholls (2nd), H. Ward (3rd) and F. Laynes (trainee). Mrs. Penn, the head cleaner had been there for 19 years and Mrs. Edith Purslow, head usherette, who had worked there for 11 years. Mrs. Purslow was well-known locally as a first-class contralto who often sang on the stage of the cinema. The well ordered hierarchy and general smartness of those days made cinemas a suitable position for ex army men, who can be seen in old documentaries drilling the page boys and inspecting their hands for cleanliness before each performance.

One major feature of the big circuits, now almost defunct, was the Saturday morning children's club. The one in High Wycombe was no exception. In 1951, the Odeon club had 1,250 members, aged between 7 and 15, 800 of whom could be expected each week. Each child paid 6d, or nothing on his or her birthday. The programme included community singing, the words being flashed on the screen. The National Anthem was also sung, and the audience repeated the club promise to the manager which ran: 'I promise to tell the truth, to help others and to obey my parents. I promise to be thoughtful of old folks, to be kind to animals and always play the game. I promise to make this great country of ours a better place to live in.' Having affirmed their good intentions, the expectant throng would then see films specially made for them under the guidance of the Home Office, N.U.T. and the Ministry of Education, or 'U' certificates on general release. The club members also played football against other circuit teams and competed in carol singing for which the Wycombe choir won the trophy at least twice. Thus it can be said that the cinema both entertained and improved the young of a whole generation or more.

Meanwhile, resuming our history, the Majestic changed hands first to County and then to Odeon, from February, 1941. The actual name change to Odeon took place in August, 1944. Seating capacity fell to 1,280 in the sixties but it was the major redevelopment of the town centre which hastened the demise of the county's grandest cinema. The great atmospheric bowed out on 25th January, 1969 with a frivolous double bill, *Carry On Up The Khyber* plus *King Kong Escapes*. There was no closure ceremony or local fuss about the cinema, but fortunately the Wycombe Film Society recorded the Odeon in their timely documentary *The Changing Face of Wycombe*. Today a large branch of F.W. Woolworth, facing the opposite direction, ascends from the High Street. In this case, it is possible to answer that oft put question, 'What happened to the organ?' — for the Comption was subsequently transferred to Quarrendon County Secondary School in Aylesbury.

The advent of the Rex, Oxford Street, the last to open in Wycombe, was described as a remarkable reconstruction achievement by *Ideal Kinema*, on 6th January, 1938. This referred to the substantial reconstruction of the old silent cinema, the Electroscope which had closed 7 years earlier. The new cinema was described as a small de luxe super, seating 688 inclusive of the original balcony. The early kinema front of house style was replaced by a new frontage in white facings, which was a large two-way vertical blue neon Rex sign. Over the black double sets of doors an attractive canopy was provided with an interchangeable programme indicator. The old butcher's shop was transformed into a pastel coloured vestibule with an island pay box and concealed lighting immediately above the entrance doors.

Inside the auditorium, seating and carpeting was finished in flame coloured texture. Apart from a brown stipled dado rising to about four feet, the walls were finished in pink pastel shades broken towards the screen end by a framed painting of a chamois jumping over clouds. The somewhat severely modern proscenium arch was delicately relieved in pastel shades, with pink tabs to match the walls and champagne coloured screen curtains. Upstairs, the projection room had been considerably enlarged, BTH sound introduced and a re-wind room added. The new owner of the Rex was C.O. Powis, a newcomer to the business whilst the reconstruction was supervised by Kenneth Friese-Green assisted by A.C. Yates, F.S.I.

The re-opening took place on 13th December, 1937, in the presence of Guy Davenport Vernon, president of the High Wycombe Chamber of Commerce. Also present, of course, were the Rex's attendants in their smart beige and maroon uniforms and Glengarry caps. The name Rex incidentally, was chosen to mark the recent coronation of George VI. Apart from films, the first of which for the record was *I Met Him in Paris* the Rex had a stage on which variety

HIGH WYCOMBE REX
Photos: John Watsham

artistes performed. One notable performer here was crooner Al Bowlly, who was booked for the week commencing Monday, 14th April, 1941. Booked by the then proprietor, John Watsham, Bowlly was billed with Jimmy Mesene, 'the Anglo-Greek ambassador of melody'. Unfortunately, the newly appointed organist failed to accompany the entertainers to time. After struggling through 'Buddy, can you spare me a dime?' Al Bowlly lost patience, brandishing his guitar over the organist's head, saying that he was killing his act. In the interval before the second house, that organist met with a mysterious accident, never to play the Rex again. However, a local church organist managed to fill the breach. Sadly the story had a tragic sequel. Al Bowlly after returning home to his Jermyn Street, London home, was killed by the blast of a Luftwaffe land mine. After a decent interval, Jimmy Mesene continued at the Rex alone, re-writing his act as a tribute to Al.

As with the Odeon, major town centre redevelopment precipitated the demise of this cinema. It closed with 566 seats on 30th January, 1965 after the screening of *Flight from Ashiya* and *The Secret Invasion*. However, demolition did not take place until 1969, after which shops occupied the site.

IVER

A village 2 miles east of Uxbridge and thus a southerly outpost of Bucks near to Greater London. Pinewood studios, named after the pine trees growing on local common land, is situated in this area.

The Plaza cinema was built facing what was Upper Wellesley Road, just south of Iver railway station. The developers were Richings Park Estate (1928) Ltd. whose estate to the south had begun some six years before the Plaza opened in 1928. The architect George E. Clare designed a Tudor style exterior, for his basically one floor 580 seat cinema. There was a small balcony provided for the Duke and Duchess of Kent, who then lived in Iver village. How often they attended is not recorded. The General Purposes Committee of the County Council insisted that the motor generator be positioned at least 10 feet from the cinema, hence it was sited in an outside basement.

The opening day was on 6th August, 1928, but unfortunately the very fine Compton organ was not ready for playing until the autumn. However, the audience did see Jacqueline Logan in *The Leopard Lady* on the Bulman Jupiter screen. There was a 25 x 35 feet stage enabling variety acts to be booked. The general manager and musical director — a grand title for a village cinema! — was a Mr. K.A. Biene, whose father composed the piece entitled *Broken Melody*. The proprietors were Mr. Sandiford and subsequently G. Norrish of Chiswick Productions Cinemas Ltd. The Plaza not only included a small cafe in which morning coffee was served by Miss Darsley, but also Standwick's photographic studio.

Soon after opening, business was helped by the closure of the Palace, Slough for redecoration, during which time the Plaza organised a bus from MacKenzie Street, Slough, departing at 5.45 and 7.45, and buses were also used

IVER PLAZA The imposing Tudoresque frontage c 1934
Photo: Mrs Brum

to bring in patrons from as far as West Drayton. However, an attempt to circumvent committee disapproval of Sunday films by creating a Sunday film club was refused in July, 1929. During weekdays the price of admission was 2/4d, 1/10d, 1/3d and 6d, or 1/3d and 6d for matinees. Despite a promising start, competition from neighbouring urban super cinemas began to bite, and when the War came, Mr. Norrish decided to use the building for the profitable purpose of storing furniture. (In the War years restrictions on moving furniture applied). The caretaker, Mrs. Brum, who had a flat in the building, and doubled up as porter at the railway station, remembers a fine white Bechstein piano being stored in what was the ladies cloakroom. There were also wireless sets kept there by McMichaels. Sadly, the Compton organ, which had been played by Doric Hawkswood, was ruined by water damage. The Plaza was finally demolished in 1962. A block of flats (Wellesley Court) occupies the site of the adjacent pebbly piece of waste land which the cinema had called the car park. The very last film shown in this short-lived cinema was *Desert Love* starring Charles Boyer.

MARLOW

A Thames-side town whose stock postcard view shows the church and the 1832 suspension bridge.

The Palace cinema, later King George's and finally the County, stood in Spittal Street roughly where the new Pickfords travel shop is today. It was by all accounts somewhat primitive, particularly in its early years. Dating from 1914, the Palace was built on the site of a blacksmith's forge. Until renamed the King George's in January, 1926, the stark interior was furnished by wooden benches on a bare board floor, and the screen was painted on the wall. It closed on 4th January, 1926 re-opening on the 28th as the King George's after improvements including tip-up seating, carpeted gangways, cork flooring, a screen with velvet curtains masked by a false proscenium arch, and equally important, a new flickerless projector. The first film to be shown in the revamped cinema was the memorable Valentino classic, *The Sheik*.

Sound was installed and the name changed to County when the circuit formed in 1929 took over the management. A scheme to rebuild on the site was mooted but eventually dropped in favour of an entirely new cinema. It is a comment on the vastly improved comfort of the new County Cinema, that in its first 6 months, press adverts carried the slogan 'only the name remains the same'. The old County closed on Wednesday, 12th January, 1938, but not before Marlow had seen *Camille*, starring Greta Garbo and Robert Taylor. Marlow's first cinema, which seated 324, was subsequently demolished.

Marlow's new County Cinema opened on the following Friday, 14th January, 1938. It was built in Station Road only 16 feet away from the Hanoverian mansion known as Marlow Place, hence its restrained "Modern Georgian" style. There was also the consideration that most patrons would be attending after dark, so excessive elaboration would have been superfluous. The cinema was designed by David Evelyn Nye, who had recently been engaged on the circuit's rebuilt County cinema at Fleet. The front elevations are of cherry coloured brick and Portland stone, and the building is set back from the road with a forecourt. However, further parking space was provided to the rear, bearing in mind the relative affluence of the local patrons. The entrance is through four pairs of double doors into a foyer with curving rear walls housing integral sales kiosk and pay box. This area is provided with lighting concealed in inverted saucer-shaped coving. There is a balcony lounge overhead reached by a curved staircase. The projection room spans the width of the balcony with administrative offices and projectionists' rest room on opposite sides. A plan of the building is retained by the County Archives Office in Aylesbury, incidentally. Another point of architectural interest is that the roofing was of pitched asbestos sheeting over a structural steel framework. Sheeting was both lighter and cheaper than tiles, costing 2/4¼d per square yard in 1938 compared with tiles at £6. 2s. 6d. per 1,000. Another price statistic one can glean from Laxton's Price book is that craftsmen working on the building would have been paid on Grade A3, that is, 1/5½d per hour compared with labourers on 1/1¼d per hour, (Marlow pay-rates).

The opening night was somewhat marred by a misunderstanding as to the number of unreserved seats available, especially as some queue jumpers took a number of them from more patient cinema-goers. Some 760 people, 258 of them in the balcony, were present for the opening film, *Victoria the Great* starring Anna Neagle. The opening ceremony was performed by British character actress Enid Stamp Taylor (1904-46) with the band and trumpeters of the Queen's

MARLOW COUNTY
Photos: Kevin Wheelan

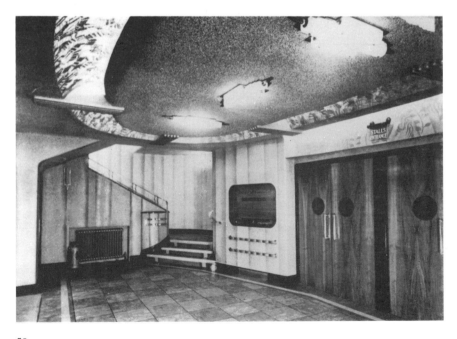

Bays, the 2nd Dragoon Guards live in support. Perhaps the most disappointed person on that day must have been Miss Gwendoline Shipton, who had been the cashier at the old cinema, but had not been re-engaged. Despite a petition in her support, neither County Cinemas nor their new local manager C.T. Mitcham felt able to reverse their decision. One director, R.S. Bromhead, who was present on the first night, praised Miss Taylor for coming down to Marlow, when so many lesser stars would have refused to leave the West End.

The new County was well favoured during the War years. Although not the head office of the Oscar Deutsch circuit, which had recently acquired the cinema, the County did benefit from the proximity of 300 circuit staff at Cookham, being the nearest house to try out new releases on the public. Famous wartime exiles in the audience included the moderniser of Albania, King Zog, who was resident locally for a time. As the cinema was not designed for stage performances, the boards were a mere 12 feet deep, and there were no dressing rooms. Thus it was that during the War when variety was included, famous people like Arthur Askey could be seen sprinting from a makeshift green room in the boilerhouse into the cinema through a fire exit! The name changed from County to Odeon on 3rd February, 1941, under which name the cinema ran until Odeon disposed of it to an independent in 1959. In the fifties there was quite a thriving patronage from local children, for the *Bucks Free Press* records that no less than 783 Christmas presents were placed around the 1957 Christmas tree to be forwarded to Dr. Barnardo's Homes.

Today, the Regal is remarkably little changed, containing many original fittings, although of necessity there is a larger screen, modern projection equipment and a new boiler. Since 22nd March, 1959, the Regal has been connected to the nearby independent Regal at Henley of similar size. There are now 622 seats, that is, 364 in the stalls, 258 in the balcony. Originally the auditorium decor was green, silver and gold, but nowadays the decor is played down by low level lighting during the intervals. There are nightly performances, with a matinee on Saturdays.

Planners have turned down a plan to replace the Regal with an office block because it would have overshadowed Marlow Place. The cinema's prospects are not good in the long term, however.

MILTON KEYNES

The largest of Britain's post-war towns, incorporating Bletchley, Stony Stratford and Wolverton (see pages 21 and 70) plus the surrounding villages. Central Milton Keynes consists of a half mile long covered shopping centre, civic buildings and clusters of low rise housing.

Although we have covered the three main towns within the new city elsewhere, there continue to be plans for an entertainment complex in the central area, near the shopping centre. In June, 1979, a plan by Granada Theatres to build a £1 million complex at Saxon Gate was announced. It would have included two cinemas, bingo hall, restaurants, a night club, plus squash club, pub, discotheque and several leisure orientated shops, had the company proceeded. Milton Keynes Development Corporation, who are actively promoting Milton Keynes as a place to live or site one's factory, are still trying to interest the major leisure companies in providing facilities for the city centre, including cinemas, but meantime, the Studio and Electra are providing the film entertainment for a population never contemplated when they were constructed.

The Development Corporation issued a news release on 20th July, 1983, announcing that an 80-feet high crystal pyramid would be the glittering landmark for a 21st century entertainment centre. A joint venture between Bass Leisure and American Multi-Cinema, who already have 720 screens, the complex will house between 10 and 23 mini-cinemas, a disco, bars and restaurants, a bingo and social club and children's entertainments. 250 employees would be needed for the 100,000 square feet of floor space, the building holding 6,000 people at a time.

Sited just off the main shopping centre along Midsummer Boulevard, patrons would approach the multi-level entertainment area through an air conditioned atrium with lush landscaping. The design concept is the work of Neil Tibbatts in partnership with Alex Stevenson of Building Design Partnership, Manchester.

This bold and imaginative centre should be built in 1985 and would be capable of screening every major release in the UK simultaneously, using several auditoria to present popular films.

NEWPORT ELECTRIC The proportioned exterior of the Electra taken in December 1980
Photo: Martin Tapsell

NEWPORT PAGNELL

A town on the River Ouzel which has successfully prevented its industry intruding on its attractive centre.

The Electra Cinema at 12 St. John Street is of exceptional interest, being the oldest cinema still on films left in the county, and also continuously managed by the same family. It opened as the Electric Theatre on 12th December, 1912 seating 585 and was the first building locally to have electric light. The foyer and manager's accommodation are contained in a Georgian doctor's house. The main building is constructed of red brick and was built in the former garden of the house. Exits were made in the garden walls for departing patrons. The roof has a cast iron frame with a wooden top coated in tiles. Originally patrons for the stalls had a separate entrance up a passage to the right of the screen, where a blocked-up pay box is still visible near the "gents". The intimate auditorium now seats 440, the small balcony supported on cast iron pillars being no longer used due to fire regulations. One supporting pillar divides the central gangway, which is lit by a spotlight during performances to avoid patrons colliding with it!

Stage performances were held periodically, one early one being Haldane

Crichton's presentation of *Monty's Flapper*, a farce direct from the Apollo Theatre, London, for one night only (Tuesday, 16th September, 1919). In the local press, patrons were asked to note that 'this is a play, not a film'. The original proprietors were Messrs. Lucas and George Salmons and Alfred Bullard. The Salmons were connected with the firm later known as Aston Martin, which had in 1912 recently increased its workforce after changing increasingly to building car bodies in place of carriages. The growing population needed entertainment and, unusually, we know exactly who provided it in the early days. Apart from the above-named proprietors, there were two operators, H. Burdett and W. Sirdler, Mrs. D. Shedd, the pianist, the Misses Edith, Emily and Alice Holland, usherettes, two commissionaires, Mr. C. Dickens and Mr. Teale and finally the caretakers, Mr. and Mrs. Webb.

For big productions the pianist was augmented by a full orchestra. Sound came, on disc, as early as 1925. Up until then the staff had to improvise — for example, chains were rattled and moans heard during the showing of *The Ghost Train*. Until 1930, the projection room was in the middle of the balcony, but plans were then submitted by Mr. E.W. Tole to resite the box further back occupying part of the rewind room and the adjacent area. Up until the fifties, patrons for the balcony had to pass through the rewinding room, extinguishing their cigarettes for the left side of the balcony, or through a passage round the box to reach the larger right side. The left side held only about 20, and tall people had to watch the ceiling! In 1938, the cinema was renamed the Electra, and we know it charged between 1/6d and 8d for admission at that time, performances being held twice nightly except Tuesdays and Fridays (7.30 p.m. only) the first show being a separate one at 2.30 on Mondays and Thursdays. In 1942, Lucas Salmons became sole owner, and he was succeeded by his daughter Margaret, the present proprietor. She still lives over the foyer, accompanied by her dog, who first strayed in during the screening of *Flash Gordon* — hence his name, Flash!

In 1964, the Electra had its main entrance and facade modernised. Even then it had been open for over half a century and naturally there are a fund of stories about the old days. One concerns an old lady, who was allowed to see the silent films for nothing, in return for keeping the matinee children quiet. Sometimes the operators cut out reels in the afternoon, hoping nobody would notice! One presumes they might have cut the love interest and left in the action, but the old lady would stay on for the second house, shouting out "they didn't do that this afternoon" when the storyline changed! Pianist Mrs. Shedd had her misfortunes. She once forgot her glasses and played merry tunes during a royal funeral newsreel. On another occasion she was frightened away from the piano by a large spider.

Today, the Electra retains a loyal audience, especially among children, who have their Saturday cinema club complete with annual outing. During the school holidays, it is normal for the cinema to be full or else very busy no matter how many performances are held. For example, in 1981, 15,000 people saw *Snow White and the Seven Dwarfs*, but it was estimated that a further 5,000 would have come had not bookable seats been sold out. Over Christmas, the auditorium is transformed over a three-day period. There is a 7 feet tree in the foyer with 80 bulbs, the kiosk becomes a fairy grotto and the ceiling becomes festooned with streamers and lanterns. A further 500 feet of streamers go up in the auditorium and the Christmas tree lights are connected to the house lights. At Christmas there is an annual children's party and film show for Aston Martin Lagonda Ltd., and everyone is invited to a carol concert held by the Pentecostal church. This is a cinema which favours films with family appeal and respects traditions. The Electra is one of the few where the National Anthem is still played. However, 'The Queen' is shown before each performance, not afterwards, avoiding the undignified stampede most cinemas used to experience!

OLNEY

An extremely attractive unspoilt town in the far north of the county with many 18th century houses.

The Electric Cinema, 81 High Street began its life as the New Hall, which was built by Olney grocer, Lewis Thompson, of 9 High Street. Used initially for concerts, meetings and dances, it also saw some very agitated election meetings. Converted into a silent cinema in 1919, it was originally called the New Hall Picture House before becoming the Electric. The hall stood back about six yards from the High Street, its two front doors admitting patrons to a large vestibule which had a pay desk on the right-hand side. The projection room was built over the front porch, with an outside iron staircase. To the left of the building, an iron gate led to the proprietor's house which was a little cottage to the rear. Inside the hall, the seats which were graded in comfort started with forms - 2½d, wooden tip-ups - 6d, padded seats - 8d, and a few with arm rests on the left at the back for 1/-.

The original proprietors were Mr. and Mrs. Clifford, the latter being a lady of regal manner who played the piano accompaniment and was referred to as 'Madam Clifford'. Her playing was interrupted periodically as Mr. Clifford or Mr. Chapman, the projectionist, proceeded through the dimly lit hall to put away one reel of film in a fire-proof box under the stage and fetch the next. An interval was held during which Madam sold chocolates, sweets, etc. Despite the fire precautions, Mr. Chapman's hands were badly burned on one occasion during the showing of, would you believe, *The Eternal Flame*. Other personalities included Olney's last blacksmith, Alastair Bull, who worked in a smithy adjoining the Castle Inn before coming on to the Electric at night. There was also a "chucker-out" Sid Brundle, whose word was law, and who only gave one warning before expelling noisy children from the six o'clock Saturday house.

J.B. Poyntz acquired the cinema. He is perhaps better known in Oxford, where he acquired the Scala, now Phoenix, in June, 1930. He disliked patrons eating chocolates, ice-cream, etc., in the auditorium, saying that people should be able to sit and watch a picture in peace. Whether he actually forbade sales is not recorded, but his two large bulldogs are still remembered walking around by queueing patrons. In 1927, there were plans to extend the hall bringing seating capacity up to 286, but the General Purposes Committee were not happy that the exit passages were only 2 feet 9 inches at their narrowest. Next year, however, a new floor was put in and a new operating and rewinding room built over the main entrance. The previous sheet-iron structure had failed to please the Committee. Mr. Poyntz sold the cinema to Mr. Webster, a film distributor, who brought films to the Electric early enough for a coach to be run twice weekly from Newport Pagnell. However, the cinema was one of the first to close when Mr. Webster moved away from the area, and the last programme shown was Fred Astaire in *Three Little Words* on 28th June, 1952. Until recently, the premises were used by a boot and shoe manufacturers, Sudborough and Wood, but of late the Electric, perhaps more appropriately, has become a lampshade factory.

PRINCES RISBOROUGH PRINCES The heavily placarded exterior
Photo: Len Wright

PRINCES RISBOROUGH

A modest sized town between Aylesbury and High Wycombe. Its historical sounding name derives from the Black Prince, who once resided in the district.

There is some evidence, which I have been unable to confirm from local from the present Walsingham Hall. The brewery itself stood on the Market Square, from the present Walsingham Hall. The brewery itself on the Market Square, but disappeared some 50 years ago. Any films shown in the hall would have been shown during and after the First World War, but ceased with the advent of the Princes Cinema (see below).

The Princes Cinema, named after the town, stood at the junction of Wycombe and Station roads. Older people still remember going there, although it too closed pre-World War II. The building was originally a British School, but became a cinema known as the Chaplin for a few months before being taken over in 1923 by the Wright family from the Isle of Wight. Mrs. Wright and her two teenage sons ran the cinema throughout its existence. Originally there were about 230 Windsor chairs in the hall, the rear ones slightly raised above the rest, facing a screen at the junction end of the hall. These seats could be removed from their battens to enable dances and other functions requiring floor space to take place. The school windows were covered by red curtaining, and the sole form of heating was a stove along the left-hand side of the room near the grand piano.

The Wright family made most of the improvements in the Princes themselves. These included constructing a new projection box at the junction end, and re-positioning the screen at the opposite end. Tip-up seats were installed reducing the capacity to about 180, but the Wrights did not flinch from unscrewing these when the floor was needed. A proscenium arch was constructed from silver coated boxes, which served as the base for columns linked by wooden trellis work. This was illuminated during the intervals very effectively by rows of bulbs shining through tinted cellophane, which would be activated in sequence. The West End blockbusters were not necessarily the films most appreciated in Princes Risborough, when they finally arrived. Such stalwarts as John Wayne, "Duke" and Laurel and Hardy ensured good attendances. Films were delivered by motor van, and such was the honesty of the times that the hiring fee could be left out on top of the heavy cases for collection. Films ran either all week or from Thursday to Saturday, depending on the time of year. At Saturday matinees, pupils from Bledlow orphanage were admitted free of charge. One blind boy managed to accompany the silent films, being told what music to play as the film progressed. The boy was known to comment on which films he had enjoyed, although how he took in the content is a mystery. There is also the story of another pianist who cycled over from Beaconsfield to play. One hot day, a new trade rep looked in a side door, opened to ventilate the hall, and asked: 'Are you the cinema?' To which the musician replied: 'No, I'm the piano!' Other regulars at the Princes were members of the O.T.C. who came from Little Kimble rifle range. These well spoken gentlemen made straight for the cheapest seats — the sixpennies. They were known for their harmless japes, which included on one occasion, projecting silhouettes on to the screen to join in the action! Seats at the Princes were bookable, but one regular courting couple received an additional service. The arm between their usual tip-up seats were sawn off by the management so that they could watch the screen in greater proximity! The Wright brothers also turned their hands to pumping the bellows of a hired organ on one occasion during the showing of a religious epic.

After the Carlton cinema (see below) opened its doors nearer the town centre, business inevitably dropped at the Princes. In 1938, the licence was renewed for only a further quarter, so we presume it closed for films around March of that year. The last film was, rather ironically, Gracie Fields in *The Show Much Go On*. The cinema then had a new Canadian maple floor laid, and enjoyed a new lease of life as a skating rink, featuring roller hockey, which drew teams from surrounding towns. All this stopped in the War however, when the building was requisitioned for War manufactures. Since that conflict, the Princes has been a printing works, and is currently little altered externally as the premises of Naylor's Insert Services.

The Carlton, Bell Street, stood opposite the present British Legion Hall. Cyril White's book 'The Past 50 Years: Princes Risborough and District Royal British Legion, 1927-1977', published in 1980, contains a distant view of the Carlton through the scaffolding of the new Legion Hall. This shows the Carlton had a rather plain brick frontage, broken by six windows, with the ground floor extended forwards towards the street. Aylesbury provided both the architect C.H. Wright and the builders, Messrs. Fleet and Roberts. The interior decoration was executed by Allied Guilds of Birmingham from a colour scheme by E.C. Whaler. Autumn tints in fawn and nile green predominated. Beside the proscenium arch were two fibrous plaster imitation organ grilles painted in platinum gold. The dado was azure blue with an overglaze of Pearl.

The Carlton seated 450, 130 of these in the balcony. The proprietor was a local solicitor John S. Stevenson, who was later joined by R.L. Weller who was already in the cinema trade. The Carlton became part of their mini circuit, which also included the Picture House, Beaconsfield and the Broadway, Chalfont St. Peter, all managed at one time by a Mr. Pitt. The Carlton opened on Monday, 15th March, 1937. The author is not aware of any stage shows taking place, but there was a Labour Party political meeting in the cinema during which special films were shown on 21st July, 1946. In 1949, Mr. A. Ayres of Baldock took over and remained there until closure took place on 8th March, 1961. The last film screened was *Beat Girl* followed by a brief spell of bingo and then a fire. The new owners were Peter Ockford Ltd. of Oxford, who bought not only the cinema but ¾ acre of land and the Carlton manager's bungalow. The last manager, K.R. Stokes, moved out as soon as his new house was completed. Subsequently, the Carlton was demolished and the block of flats known as Carlton Court built on the site. An interesting parallel here with Tring, where a similar sized cinema has now been replaced by Regal Court.

SLOUGH

Athough now a Berkshire town, which I hope one day will be covered in a history of that county's cinemas, a brief resume of what were Buckinghamshire cinemas might interest the reader.

In Windsor Road, where Renacres (ironmongers) now stands, there was the Little Gem Bioscope, later known as the Crown Cinema, but unofficially as the "Flea Pit". Demolished ca. 1927-28. The Empire Cinema Palace, or Electric, stood in Chalvey Road, occupying a deconsecrated chapel built in 1838. As a cinema it functioned from around 1912-24, and it was subsequently a working mens' club, newsagents, dolls' hospital and now Cooper's Off Licence. The Adelphi, Bath Road, designed by Eric Norman Bailey of Maidenhead, was a cinema between 17th February, 1930 and 21st January, 1973. Owned by ABC and then Granada it had a large stage and ballroom, but is now used for bingo. The Cinema Palace, 161 High Street opened in July, 1911 next to a roller skating rink. Closed in the Great War it was derelict until incorporated into Harris Motor Garage in August, 1922. Isaac's furniture store stands on the site, at 251 High Street. Another Palace at 127/29 High Street behind Purser's butchers shop, opened on 1st September, 1921. It was burnt out on V.J. Night (1945). Reconstructed afterwards it was the Century Cinema from 1949 until 26th January, 1957. Now a Waitrose supermarket. The Ambassador, Farnham Road was a cinema from 17th February, 1936 until 10th February, 1968 when it went over to Top Rank bingo. Out in Cippenham, there was the Commodore, opened in November, 1938 with an organ. Run by Essoldo, it switched to bingo around 1965. Lastly there is the Granada, still on films, and boasting a Wurlitzer organ first played by Dudley Beaver. Situated in Windsor Road, the Granada opened on 23rd March, 1938 with *It's Love I'm After* and remains on films as a triple (from June, 1973). Once it boasted of 2,001 armchairs, but now seats 624, 261 and 197 patrons in Screens 1 to 3. I have not researched Slough, but my thanks to Reg Harrison, who provided much of the above information. (Extra reference: Ambassador Cinema. See Ideal Kinema, March, 1936).

STONY STRATFORD

A town that has retained many distinctive buildings of character despite being on the north west fringe of the Milton Keynes conurbation.

The exact opening date of the Scala, Wolverton Road, Stony Stratford is not known, but it is thought to have opened shortly after the Great War, certainly by 1921. The cinema should not be confused with a smaller theatre, known as the Empire, which stood next to the tram sheds. The Scala, until ca. 1938, seated 700 inclusive of the balcony, the cheapest seats being hard wooden benches. A separate entrance and pay box for the latter was manned for many years by a Mr. Maycock. One of his duties was to eject the youthful perpetrators of undue disturbances. A favourite boyish prank in this category was to stuff a firework through the ventilation grille attached to a slow burning saltpetre fuse, then enter the cinema and sit down to await the ensuing bangs. No doubt the management got wise to this escapade in due course! Not much can be said about the Scala's interior, which was unremarkable. There were cream or blue hardboard walls and ceilings, with black painted slats at the joins. The effect must have been not unlike a mock Tudor tea room or a Stratford on Avon launderette. More unusual, for a purpose-built cinema, there was rear projection, with a fifty feet throw to the screen. Outside, the Scala had a castellated and stepped gable roof with a modest entrance flanked by two smallish windows.

In silent days, attendances were good, although until 1926, patrons could take a short tram ride to two more cinemas in Wolverton. Silent films of any distinction were made more realistic by people behind the screen making sound effects. Those accompanying *The Four Horsemen of the Apocalypse* were said to have been particularly effective, no doubt including several coconut shells! Later in 1936, 1,300 people crowded in to the two separate Saturday houses to witness the film of King George V's funeral. They overflowed into the gangways breaking all the safety regulations. Although in the same circuit, the Palace Wolverton was separately booked, except that the *Gaumont British News* was shared. This was shown first at the Palace and then brought by bus to the Scala for inclusion later in the evening. If late, the projectionist had to make some hasty re-arrangement of the film schedule. The usherettes, who wore a maroon uniform with gold epaulettes, did not confine themselves to gesturing patrons to their seats or selling Eldorado ice-cream. They also, in turns, closed the curtains at the end of performances by hand. Electrical equipment was mooted but never installed. Mains electricity too was late in coming, as a gas engine provided the power until it broke down irrevocably in 1937.

As at the Palace, the first proprietor was Alderman Barber, the cinema pioneer from Staffordshire. The Moss family managed the two cinemas and later leased them. Tommy Moss managed the Scala, and his son, Johnny, the Palace. The Moss residence was a large mansion called the White House, which stood until it made way for the present United Counties bus station. It had half an acre of land for the upkeep of which the Moss family employed a gardener. In 1937, the Moss family sank capital into a new cinema in Cranfield, Bedfordshire, a venture which proved too expensive and they subsequently sold out to Basingham Theatres. At this time, the last of the benches were removed and seating capacity reduced to 558 in tip-ups. Basingham Theatres had the praiseworthy custom of paying a bonus to their staff if the net profit exceeded £120 per week, which it often did. The projectionist would receive an extra 7/6d and usherettes about 3/6d. Although the Scala had no dressing rooms, there was a reasonable stage, which was used during the War for talent shows. However, it is doubtful if the occupants of the rear stalls, who were thoughtfully provided with double seats, noticed the difference!

After the War, several managers tried to make the Scala pay in increasingly difficult circumstances. In November, 1952, H.V. Prince received the licence in succession to T.A. Broome. Like Mr. Walter Gay in Beaconsfield, Mr. Prince turned a blind eye to children seeing certain 'A' films, but was eventually dissuaded by police intervention! In July, 1955 the Scala closed briefly after the demise of F.W. Allwood Theatres, to Basingham Theatres, but was rescued by E.V. Thomasen, a motor engineer and motor insurance assessor. Mr. Thomasen was saddled with some of the debts of his predecessors (see section on Wolverton) but late in 1960 he died. When, early in 1961, the General Purposes Committee had received no application to renew the licence, they ordered the closure of both the Scala and the Palace. Both went dark with the stills for next week's film in place. At Stony Stratford, the last film seen by the probably unsuspecting last nighters was *The Day They Gave Babies Away* (remember that one?) which was shown on Saturday, 22nd January, 1961. *Cash McCall* never reached the screen.

Today, the Scala can be found standing well back from the main road surrounded by cars, next door to the aforementioned bus station. It has been used as a motor supplies store, currently Newport Pagnell Tyres and Exhausts. The clock, now defunct, above the doors postdates the cinema era. There was a fire in 1980 which damaged the interior and burnt through the roof, so there is little of the cinema pedigree visible. Walls and roof, which once echoed to the dialogue of Hollywood stars, now provide shelter for large piles of motor tyres.

WINSLOW

A small town between Aylesbury and Buckingham with many Georgian buildings. In 1892, what was to become the Oddfellows Hall was built at the instigation of Mr. Chinnery, of Winslow Hall. Rather typical of the early corrugated iron village hall, with a gabled porch entrance, the building was originally used mainly for young peoples' gymnastics. In 1921, however, the Oddfellows moved from their old premises in Horn Street, known as the Iron Room. Film shows began in 1921, initially three times a week, but just Fridays and Saturdays by 1935. Two successive proprietors were Cyril Hall, then Mr. R.J. Fountaine, a photographer of 42 High Street, Aylesbury.

By all accounts, the building was not ideal for films, having wooden and concrete floors on varying levels, and draughty doors which combatted the

WINSLOW ODDFELLOWS HALL taken in 1975
Photo: Buckinghamshire Advertiser

efforts of the overhead electric heaters in winter. The projection room was sited over the entrance hall and the General Purposes Committee sanctioned a second machine subject to accommodation being provided for rewinding films. Films ceased during the Second World War when the hall was used as an evacuee centre and drill hall, but thereafter the hall passed to a Public Hall Committee who showed films on Friday nights.

In July, 1947, the first plans to re-open the cinema facility were rejected by the General Purposes Committee of the County Council on the grounds that the premises did not meet the required standards. More specifically, there were too few exits, the projection box was unsatisfactory, there was no rewinding room and because of other functions, the seating was not bolted to the floor. It is presumed that sufficient improvements were made to satisfy the Committee as local sources say that films were shown until about 1956, although these were not advertised in the local press. The cinema finally closed because it failed to meet the fire regulations, and the hall was partially demolished during rebuilding carried out in 1974. The last vestiges of the original hall vanished after a fire in May, 1976.

WOLVERTON

A Victorian town of red brick terraced streets with quite a distinctive architectural and social character. It expanded around the LNWR works where railway carriages are still made.

It is easy to knock bingo, but quite a number of cinemas owe their survival to the popularity of this game. The players who cast their eyes down on score cards in Zetters' Leisure and Social Club, Wolverton, occupy a very historic property. Barber's Electric Picture Palace, Stratford Road, was second in North Bucks only to the Palace (later County) at Fenny Stratford. The former opened on Monday, 18th December, 1911. Consultation with Stratford & Wolverton RDC's surveyor had been left to the last minute, and the plans were only made available to the council on 24th October, when the Palace was no doubt well under way, structurally. The proprietor, Alderman Barber, was born in Congleton in 1860, and as a pioneer exhibitor in Britain rose to be chairman of the North Staffs Cinema Exhibitors Association and Lord Mayor of Stoke. A curious incident took place during the construction of the cinema. A horse, which had died nearby, was conveniently buried in the foundations — we know this today as a man who witnessed the internment still comes to the building to play bingo over the grave.

All went well on the opening day, although the heating did not function during the first week. Starting off with the 3,200 feet "epic" *Zigomar*, the Palace made a big impact under its manager Johnny Moss, aided by pianist Oliver Thorneycroft, who was later to become musical director of the Empire, Kingston. Variety turns were booked between the films. One of the latter was well timed. As 40,000 men of the recently modernised British Army visited North Bucks on manoeuvres (1913), the film *The Battle of Paardeburg* was shown. There were matinees on Saturdays for children, who were enticed to

WOLVERTON PALACE   The venerable and unpretentious exterior
Photo: Martin Tapsell

the first one with a free stick of Blackpool rock on 23rd December, 1911. Adult admission cost between 3d and 9d, to the cinema that was 'well ventilated, with ample exits, and sprayed daily with Jeyes fluid'. Programmes were changed on Mondays and Thursdays. The licensee even tried to get a Christmas Day licence in 1913, but was refused.

The Palace, which seated 650, inclusive of a medium sized balcony, stayed open for nearly half a century. Its history is shared with the sister cinema in Stony Stratford. We might add here that when F.W. Allwood Theatres went out of business in 1955, they owed £243. 5s. to the County Council for the Sunday entertainment charitable levy. This worked out at 1d a seat to charity if the cinema opened on Sundays. Mr. E.V. Thomasen who took over both the Scala and the Wolverton Palace, offered to pay the debt off in monthly instalments but was soon in difficulties. Mr. Thomasen died late in 1960, so that the Palace suffered the same fate of sudden closure on 22nd January, 1961 as the Scala at Stony Stratford. In Wolverton's case the last film was *The Tattered Dress* and Wolverton did not see *Doctor In Love* the next week.

Today, as mentioned above, the historic building is a Zetters' Social Club, after being a dance hall for a while. The frontage is windowless, of rendered brick, with two exit doors from the proscenium end taking one straight on to the pavement. Bingo players use a side entrance leading to a small entrance with facing pay box. The interior retains much atmosphere from the early days. All but the outer pairs of cinema seats in the stalls have been replaced by cafeteria style seating. The balcony is still used, and there are 116 tip-up seats still in place. The sides of the balcony curve round to two narrow passages leading in theatrical fashion to exit stairs beside the proscenium arch. The projection box is reached up the main stairs, but apart from two ports, the small room retains little of interest to the cinema enthusiast. However, there is an impressive fireplace in the upstairs bar, and next door in a storage area, an even more intriguing door panel with a heraldic crest resembling a chained ram and the motto supra 'Crom a boo' — the motto meaning 'Crom for ever' is the ancient war-cry of the Irish clan of Fitzgerald, referring to Crom castle in County Limerick. Its connection, if any, to Wolverton is alas, forgotten. The club, which is a busy one, is open daily from 1.30 p.m. and again in the evenings.

Wolverton's postal sorting office, formerly the Empire Cinema, has an interesting past. At the beginning of the century, there was a row of cottages on

WOLVERTON EMPIRE The original Empire.
Photo: Kevin Wheelan

72

WOLVERTON NEW EMPIRE Taken c1937.
Photos: Kevin Wheelan

WOLVERTON NEW EMPIRE Projection box
Photo: Kevin Wheelan

the site which were converted into shops during the First World War and a toy factory added at the back. Fred Tilley's toys sold well until after the Great War when German competition resumed. It was then decided to convert the factory's paint shop on the first floor into a concert hall with stage facilities, with a dance hall below. The two uses conflicted and in May, 1923 the building was closed after the staging of the revue *Ship Ahoy* for alterations to enlarge the stage and bring the seating capacity up to 800. Either at this stage or in 1926 when films were introduced, the building was completely gutted to make the two floors one hall. When the Empire became mainly a cinema, Fred Tilley relinquished control. The cinema was equipped with rear projection with a 30 feet throw to a translucent screen.

During its first year on films, the Empire was used as a centre for workmen involved in the 1926 General Strike, which of course, affected the railway works. In the autumn of 1932, further alterations took place and seating capacity was reduced on at least two occasions — in 1938 when part of the balcony was partitioned off for storage, and in 1949 when the rear rows in the stalls were taken out, cutting capacity from 620 to 539. The proprietors until 1933 were the Southan Morris circuit who merged with Union Cinemas in 1933, Mr. Morris becoming general manager of Union Cinemas. In October, 1937, Union Cinemas were linked to ABC, but as ABC found many of the Union acquisitions were not very profitable, the Empire was one of the cinemas disposed of to an independent. The disposal took place in 1939.

After the War the Empire competed for a declining share of cinema business with the Palace, until the latter's sudden demise in 1961. Shortly afterwards, in February, 1961 the Empire announced that it had acquired 170 reconditioned seats (from the Palace perhaps?) and also some reconditioned sound apparatus. 'For good pictures, warmth and comfort, visit the Empire cinema' the advert advised. The public failed to take note in sufficient numbers, as the owners, London and Provincial cinemas sold the building to the Ministry of Works for a future Post Office sorting office extension. Consequently, the cinema owners, now lessees, were reluctant to spend money on improvements. In 1969, as the lease was running out, it was decided to close down. Two Carry On films made up the double closing bill on 17th May, 1969 — *Carry On Screaming* and *Carry On Cleo* after which the staff locked up for the last time. Among those affected were manageress Joyce Harper, and the projectionists Tony Mills and John Tompkins.

In many cases when a cinema closes, local people may not have the opportunity to salvage anything of practical or sentimental value. At the Empire, however, various relics were available — they included seats at 10/- each, fire extinguishers at £2 and a kiosk with shelves. Maybe some of them are still to be found in Wolverton homes — who knows? The gable of the old cinema is just visible above the bland exterior of the sorting office, but to enter Wolverton's former entertainment buildings today you need to be a postman, or a bingo player.

WYCOMBE ELECTROSCOPE THEATRE

ALWAYS THE BEFORE YOU

We have the honour to announce that THE WORSHIPFUL

THE MAYOR OF HIGH WYCOMBE

COUNCILLOR RICHARD T. GRAEFE, ESQ., J.P.,

WILL OPEN THIS THEATRE

ON

Wednesday, Feb. 28th, 1912.

The Main Entrance in Oxford Street will be opened by HIS WORSHIP with a SOLID GOLD Presentation KEY at **7** p.m.

SPECIAL GRAND PROGRAMME : : : **7.45** p.m.
To commence precisely at

Many well known local Ladies and Gentleman will be Present

SPECIAL PRICES THIS NIGHT ONLY 2/-, 1/6, 1/- and 6d. Limited Number.

The whole of the Receipts will be given to the COTTAGE HOSPITAL.

"SIMS' VAUDEVILLE ORCHESTRA." Programs Free.

NOTE: ORDINARY TIMES IN FUTURE AS FOLLOWS:

MATINEES DAILY: DOORS OPEN 2.30 COMMENCE 2.45
(MONDAYS & THURSDAYS EXCEPTED)
TO WHICH LADIES & CHILDREN ARE SPECIALLY INVITED

6.30 TWICE·NIGHTLY 8.45
COMMENCING SHARP

SATURDAYS DOORS OPEN AT 6.15 & 8.40

CHILDREN'S SPECIAL GRAND MATINEE
EVERY SATURDAY DOORS OPEN 2 SHARP REDUCED PRICES

POPULAR PRICES 1s. 6d., 1s., 6d., and 3d.